Rewire Your Anxious Brain:
Stop Overthinking, Find Calm, and Be Present

by Nick Trenton

www.NickTrenton.com

Table of Contents

PART ONE: UNDERSTANDING HOW ANXIETY WORKS   7

CHAPTER 1: THE CYCLE OF ANXIETY   7

CHAPTER 2: UNWINDING THE ANXIETY HABIT LOOP   23

CHAPTER 3: CHANGE YOUR SOUNDTRACK   37

PART TWO: UNRAVELING THE ANXIETY RESPONSE   53

CHAPTER 4: THE ANXIETY TIMELINE   53

CHAPTER 5: THE ABCDE METHOD   67

CHAPTER 6: MANAGING EXPECTATIONS   81

PART THREE: YOUR BRAIN—FRIEND OR FOE?   99

CHAPTER 7: COGNITIVE DISTORTIONS AND THE TRIPLE COLUMN TECHNIQUE   99

CHAPTER 8: REALITY TESTING   113

PART FOUR: TAKING A STEP BACK   129

CHAPTER 9: THE BATMAN EFFECT   129

CHAPTER 10: LEARNING TO TOLERATE UNCERTAINTY   141

CHAPTER 11: EXTERNALIZATION   153

PART FIVE: SMART STRESS MANAGEMENT TOOLS   169

CHAPTER 12: MIND MAPPING   169

CHAPTER 13: BETTER DECISION-MAKING MEANS LESS ANXIETY   181

CHAPTER 14: TURNING YOUR ANXIETY INTO A SUPERPOWER   195

SUMMARY GUIDE   211

Part One: Understanding How Anxiety Works

Chapter 1: The Cycle of Anxiety

Anxiety is a funny thing. You may well know how anxiety *feels* as it's happening, but do you really know what it is? How it works?

If you're one of the millions of people who struggle with anxiety, you may have already noticed a certain irony in your position: **The more anxious you feel, the more afraid you are of that experience, and the more you try to avoid it**. But in avoiding it, you forgo the opportunity to understand exactly what is happening to you . . . and so you continue to be at its mercy. It's a little like wondering what awful thing might be hiding under the bed. So long as you never actually look to see what is there, you will never really know, and the fear will always remain big, nebulous, and completely unknown.

So, this is where we will start: by taking a good look under the bed to see what we are really dealing with.

Anxiety manifests in each individual person in completely unique ways. Your anxiety will not be like anyone else's. That said, anxiety is a common human experience that is remarkable consistent across all historical periods, peoples, and cultures. There is much we know about anxiety, from its more abstract expressions to the very real physiological symptoms, like a pounding heart and elevated blood pressure. And though your particular experience of anxiety will be unique to you, you will most likely experience it as a definite and predictable pattern—i.e., the experience unfolds in a cycle.

Knowledge is power, and the first way to gain power over anxiety is to learn its habits. You may find it far easier to deal with anxiety attacks if you recognize the signs of each of the four stages. This does two things: First, it tells you that your experience, no matter how unpleasant, *will* pass. Second, if you understand that an anxiety wave is coming, you can prepare for it and, in some cases, stand aside so the wave passes with as little damage as possible. Let's take a look at the familiar paths that the anxiety response travels.

Stage 1: Noticing anxiety and wanting to deal with it

Because it's a continuous cycle, this isn't really "Step 1," but it's a convenient place to start. This is the stage at which anxiety is triggered and an amplifying cycle is set off. A certain stimulus can start the snowball, but this stimulus doesn't necessarily have to be an objectively stressful event. It could be:

External—certain kinds of weather, sights or sounds, particular people, situations or environments, demands or challenges, something on the news, a kind of activity, or even an object.

Internal—a mental image, a memory, an idea, an internal bodily sensation, or a desire.

The anxiety trigger may be a blend of many things both external and internal. Whatever it is, this trigger causes a stress response—i.e., the famous fight-or-flight mode. All your perceptions then narrow in on this one stimulus, and you become hyper-focused on it, interpreting it as a threat (which it may or may not be).

Let's consider the example of Annie, who has begun to experience panic attacks. Her trigger is a combination of feeling too hot, constricted, or trapped. This combines with the vague internal thought "I can't escape."

Her first panic attack happened in a gym on the treadmill—she became very warm, and her shirt was too tight and constricting. Subsequent panic attacks have happened in crowded places or on overly hot public transport where she felt this same hot, cloying, claustrophobic sensation. Annie has noticed she even felt this sense of panic once when having a "heated" argument with her mother.

Stage 2: Avoidance

Your brain is smart. It wants to help you. If it's aware that something is causing distress, or it perceives something as a threat, it wants to help you survive by making sure you avoid that thing. Unfortunately, this part of your survival machinery doesn't distinguish between a real and unreal threat. **This means that you can sometimes learn**

to avoid things that are not actually a threat.

The second phase of the anxiety loop is where you learn to avoid any situations that might trigger anxiety. Avoidance can also be internal or external:

External—You may physically remove yourself from a situation. For Annie, she simply doesn't go to the gym anymore and has vowed to never get on a treadmill again. Once or twice, Annie has called in sick to work because she was worried she'd be forced to do activities in a crowd.

Internal—You may consciously remove your awareness from an idea, perhaps redirecting your attention.

For Annie, when she is forced to be on public transport, she tries hard to distract herself by squeezing her eyes shut and listening to music with earphones. She has even noticed that, for no "logical" reason, she has made a habit of little rituals she needs to do every day before leaving the house or getting out of bed. Sometimes, she needs to rehearse a special mental "game" she has created for herself, whereby if she recites a certain rhyme correctly three times, she can somehow protect herself from overwhelming negative thoughts and panic.

Stage 3: Temporary relief

All these avoidance behaviors actually *do* work—but only for a time. Still, anxious people are drawn to avoidance even if its effects don't last. This is because avoidance is *negative reinforcement.* Behavioral psychology states that rewarded behavior—positive or negative—is more likely to continue. The reward for avoidance is temporary relief. You avoid the feeling and squash that rising sense of anxiety—in other words, when you are trapped in the cycle, it feels like avoidance is the solution. But, you are still in the cycle. As you can guess, stage 3 leads neatly into stage 4, which then sets you up for one more go around the loop. But in the moment, it doesn't feel like that.

In Annie's life, when she walked out of the gym and said, "I'll never get on a treadmill again," she actually did feel better for doing so. She felt empowered in that moment, and as though she had identified the problem (treadmills) and found a permanent solution (just don't get on one ever again). Of course, from outside of the cycle, we can see that Annie's feeling of success is somewhat of an illusion. That's because the problem is not her job or her mother or crowded buses or heat or treadmills. Her problem is the *entrenched anxiety cycle*. The best that avoidance can ever do is help you temporarily escape a trigger. But the anxiety itself is still there, still running through its motions.

Stage 4. Returning to a state of heightened anxiety

Let's imagine that Annie succeeds for a time with all her avoidance and "safety behaviors," but one day she is caught in an elevator with five other people on a hot summer afternoon. As you can imagine, her anxiety is reliably triggered, and she starts to feel panic. Because she is hyperfocused on the various "threatening" stimuli and has learned through many cycles of repetition that this is a Bad Thing to avoid, she immediately does her best to avoid or escape all the unpleasantness. But now she can't!

Being trapped in the elevator prevents all her normal avoidance behavior, and she doesn't have her earphones or anything else that can help distract her. So what happens? Annie has an anxiety attack. Her anxiety is back again in full force. When the elevator is fixed and the situation is finally over, she leaves the building, vowing, "I'll never step foot in an elevator again." And so, the cycle continues.

Before we continue, it's worth pointing out that anxiety doesn't need to look as extreme or clear-cut as Annie's example to "count" as an anxiety problem. You may never experience a full-blown panic attack. But that doesn't mean that your anxiety is not a problem, or that some form of the cycle isn't running, continually reinforcing a maladaptive response to stress. You do not need to have a specific phobia or OCD for anxiety to play a negative role in your life. No matter how anxiety manifests in your life, you can improve the situation by becoming familiar with these four stages and learning to see what they look like for you.

Getting Familiar with the Four Stages

Learn to identify which stage of the cycle you might be in.

The cycle can be broken at any stage, but it is easier to intervene when anxiety isn't yet off the charts and extreme. What came immediately before you started to notice anxious feelings? Were they internal or external triggers? Try to identify them in as much detail as possible.

Now become curious about the very next thing that happened. How did you respond to this initial trigger? Remember that the cycle is amplifying—it keeps building on the step before it, accelerating anxious feelings. But it may have begun in a relatively small way to a relatively minor trigger. Can you see what it was?

Your ultimate goal will be to reverse the cycle completely, but first try to just understand what is happening, and how.

Check your thoughts.

What thoughts came immediately in response to the trigger? Typically, we are responding to our *thoughts about a trigger*, and not strictly the trigger itself. If you examine yourself carefully, you may find that you have thoughts such as:

- I can't handle this
- This is bad
- I'm going to have a panic attack
- I can't cope
- I'm in danger

- Something is very wrong
- Trouble is coming and I can't avoid it
- I may become out of control
- What if . . .?

For many people who battle anxiety, there is often a lightning-fast initial response to a trigger that exaggerates the threat that trigger represents. This may be so quick it is unconscious. For Annie, feeling hot equals feeling panic. Without even realizing it, Annie has told herself again and again that this state of physiological arousal (being hot) is something bad, undesirable, uncontrollable, and dangerous. In reality, it's a neutral sensation and certainly not a threat.

This may seem like an exaggeration, but just think for a moment about the things that usually make people anxious, and ask whether they are responding to a genuinely threatening situation or to the *story they are telling themselves* about how scary that situation is. The first step is to become clear about what thoughts are setting up and maintaining the anxiety loop for you. Do you notice any pattern of overthinking, obsession, self-doubt, or catastrophizing?

Check your body.

Anxiety is never "all in the head." While the trigger may be neutral and the "threat" purely a response to a mental interpretation, that doesn't mean that your body isn't responding *as if* it were dealing with a great white shark. Our thoughts respond to anxiety and so does our body. We can change the anxiety spiral by changing our thoughts, just as we can by observing our body and taking steps to physiologically relax ourselves.

Try a body scan. This can help you pinpoint any physical response you may be experiencing:

- As though your conscious awareness were a beam of light traveling over your entire body, starting from the top and working its way down, check in with each part of yourself and notice what you feel.
- What sensations are you experiencing? Try to just *notice* rather than judge, interpret, or diagnose. Think in terms of temperature, tension, or other sensations like flutteriness, burning, queasiness, lightness, and so on. You may find that

metaphors or imagery can help you nail down the more abstract sensations (for example, "my head feels like it's full of cotton candy").
- Tune into your stomach—it's called your "second brain" for a reason. Is it tight, painful, or just feeling strange? What would it say if it could speak?
- Notice your skin (sweating, goosebumps, sensations of heat, or "pins and needles"?) as well as what your breath is doing (is your breathing shallow, deep, regular, jagged?).
- Finally, you might like to connect these sensations with some of the thoughts you've identified in yourself. In Annie's example, feeling too hot actually causes a strange sensation of iciness and tingling on her skin, as this seems to accompany the thought, "here we go again" and the feeling that she is spinning out of control.

Now reflect.

When you are trapped in the cycle, you may be speeding along from one anxious sensation to the other, and quite likely feeling out of control. But if you can reflect on the process (when you're calm and out of the cycle), you can slow down and see what is actually happening. You can see how each stage is connecting to the next stage. One final consideration is to ask how your current anxiety habits are serving you. Look at your avoidance behaviors and see if you can pinpoint the exact moment you decided to engage in them to escape the perceived threat.

But then ask how well these avoidance mechanisms have actually worked for you. How long did the sense of relief last for you? For Annie, the relief never lasts for longer than a few days or a week. Remember, as you become curious about your coping mechanisms, try not to lay blame or shame—you are trying to understand how your brain has been helping you cope. So, there's no need to feel bad that you have been using strategies that are actually worsening your anxiety in the long term. Instead, focus on feeling proud that you are learning more about yourself and giving yourself the chance to break out of patterns that are no longer working for you.

Reversing the Cycle

According to the Government of West Australia's Centre for Clinical Interventions, it's possible to break the cycle of anxiety by reversing it. To put it simply, you need to:

Step 1. Confront feared situations *without the help of unhealthy coping mechanisms* (i.e., go without your avoidance behaviors).

Step 2. After confronting your fear, give yourself permission and time to experience a short-term or slight increase in anxiety. If you are patient and persistent, your physical and mental symptoms will diminish.

Step 3. Lean into healthy coping skills to help you reduce your anxiety to a manageable level. This could be breathing and relaxation exercises (to calm the body) or changing the way you think (to calm the mind).

In time, it is perfectly possible to teach yourself new ways to respond to what were previously triggering stimuli. One way of thinking about it is to see the anxiety response as simply something you've learned—and that means it can be unlearned.

In the remainder of this book, we'll be considering each of the above steps in more detail and looking at various ways we can start to take charge of our emotional and physical responses to life. We will explore ways to unpick our anxiety habits and replace them with techniques that we have engineered to focus on our values and goals instead. We will learn to detach from this anxiety spiral, manage any triggers, and even put our tendency toward anxiety to good use where possible. But the first step is awareness. No amount of deep breathing, visualization, or journaling will help until you have a clear idea of what it is you're dealing with.

Chapter 2: Unwinding the Anxiety Habit Loop

Experiencing anxiety is not a character flaw. It's not something that you're doing wrong, and it's definitely not something that is a permanent part of your personality. Instead, it's far easier to remind yourself that **anxiety is simply a learned behavior**. When we consistently repeat a behavior, our brains store the associated response. The more we repeat, the more entrenched those associations become. Even if you've been anxious for a long time, or your associations are very deep, they are still just habits, and they *can* be changed.

When you think about it, so much of our daily life consists of these automatic habitual "loops." It's just that most of them are quite neutral—the way we make coffee in the morning, the way we get dressed, the order in which we clean the kitchen, and so on. Again, our brain is smart, and it uses this kind of autopilot thinking to help us complete essential but mundane tasks as efficiently as possible. *Habits are great.* We need habits—they are what allow us to save our mental resources for the real challenges of life.

The brain, however, does not differentiate between different kinds of information. It doesn't know that it is helping you be really, really "efficient" . . . at worrying about nothing! The brain does something that is easy and time-saving with no concern for whether it is accurate, useful, or in the interest of your overall wellbeing. In just the same way as you automatically brush your teeth every morning, you may worry and stress in endless loops. Again, this is not a character trait or a personal failing. The reason you have anxiety doesn't need to involve any heavy trauma from the past or complicated metaphysical explanations. The reason you are anxious today could be as simple as "because you were anxious yesterday."

The way you currently respond to stress is an indication of the way you have most consistently reacted to stress in the past. Once the brain has been programmed to respond in a certain way, it will continue to make connections to the same loops, even if those reactions are counterproductive in the present moment. It will continue to do it, that is, until you deliberately stop the cycle.

Automatic learning and habit cycles form in the area of the forebrain known as the basal ganglia. The three-part story of how a behavior becomes cemented as a habit goes like this:

1. A **cue** from the environment triggers you
2. You do the behavior or run through a **routine** in response
3. There is a **reward** so that the next time you encounter the cue, you remember and do the behavior again

Every single behavior that you do automatically today, good or bad, was once "programmed" via the above three steps. For example:

1. **Cue**: you see an email from your boss in your inbox

2. **Routine**: you put off opening it for as long as possible
3. **Reward**: you don't have to face whatever it is you might find in there (for a while, at least)

A reward doesn't have to be a carrot on a stick. It can sometimes be the simple avoidance of something unpleasant. Importantly, the cue, routine, and reward don't have to be genuinely linked—if we *perceive* them as linked somehow, then they are. Every time we run through the routine, that neural pathway strengthens. It gets to be so that we *never* see an email from our boss and open it immediately.

Taking Charge of the Anxiety Loop

Step 1: Map out your anxiety habits

Keep in mind that most of your anxiety habits developed as a way to *reduce* stress, even if they don't always benefit you in the long run, and even if they ultimately increase stress. The first step is to do a biopsy on your habits and identify the cue, the exact behavior itself, and the reward/consequence.

Step 2: Work with your brain's reward system

Your anxious behavior is in place because there is a reason to do it—the reward. Reward a different behavior, or stop rewarding the current one, and your behavior will change over time. The great thing is that with awareness, every moment of anxiety is actually a hidden opportunity to learn more about yourself and to grow and develop as a person.

When dealing with anxiety, you are never punishing or forcing yourself. You are working *with* your brain and not against it. You do not want to wrench yourself away from behavior that your brain considers a safety blanket—that will be painful. But you want to make it so that you naturally become dissatisfied with your old coping mechanisms and move away from them willingly without having to exert much willpower.

Step 3: Create new habits

Most suggestions for anxiety reduction only tackle this step and ignore the other two. We all know the healthy habits and behaviors we want to adopt, but we often seem unable to make the logical choice the thing we actually choose and make a habit. But consider that you are never really breaking a bad habit or eliminating it—you can never be without habits. Rather, you are always replacing bad habits with better ones. Take the habit away without giving yourself something to realistically manage stress, and you risk creating discomfort that will only have you rushing back to your old tricks, often with even more determination!

How does all this look when applied to real life? Let's go back to Annie and the case of the Terrible Treadmill.

Step 1: Annie carefully identifies a behavior she wants to change: her inability to stick with her gym goals. Cue: feeling hot on the treadmill. Behavior: quitting. Reward: a feeling of relief.
Step 2: Annie tackles the behavior on both ends. She tries to reduce the cue by making sure that she exercises under the AC vent and brings a spray bottle to keep her cool. She also reduces the reward by asking a trusted friend to hold her accountable to her gym goals. The agreement is that the friend gets one hundred dollars if she quits (not to

mention the embarrassment). This makes quitting feel like much less of a relief!

Step 3: It's not just about engineering a different response, though. Annie also creates new, healthier routines. She gives herself a healthy treat every time she completes a planned treadmill workout. Every time she does, she is creating a new pathway in her brain: treadmill equals good feelings.

Now, some of us might take exception to thinking of our behavior the same way a dog trainer thinks of an Alsatian jumping through hoops. Even though the above might seem overly simple, the truth is that so much of our habitual and automatic behavior *is* that simple. Stubborn, yes, but not overly complex.

The way to break out of these conditioned responses and habits is with mindfulness and awareness. A few tips as you work on your own "programming" and start to change some of the carrots and sticks that keep it in place:

- **Maintain awareness and a sense of curiosity:** Rather than judging yourself for being anxious, or getting

obsessed about where your anxiety is coming from, just get curious. This is answering *how* and *what* questions instead of *why* questions. What does it feel like, and where? How does it change? Get really familiar with yourself and your habits—they're nothing to be scared of!
- **Breathing:** Breath and awareness go hand in hand. Tune into the breathing sensations in your body and you automatically connect to the moment. Try breathing "into" places where anxiety shows up. For example, Annie notices that her anxiety often feels like hot and cold prickles along the skin of her back and neck. So she slows down and, with every breath, imagines that the oxygen she is inhaling is diffusing out into her skin and soothing and calming it.
- **Try the R.A.I.N. acronym:** This is a mindfulness practice where you *relax* into the present moment; *accept* and allow it to be there; *investigate* your bodily sensations, emotions, and thoughts; and *note* what is happening. For example, as Annie runs on the treadmill, she breathes deeply and evenly and relaxes, she notices that

weird hot feeling but doesn't fight it, she becomes curious about what is happening, and she simply notices it without reacting and without getting off the treadmill. She is teaching herself to be non-reactive, and learning that just because a trigger happens, it doesn't mean she *has to* respond to it.

- **Noting:** This is a practice of labeling what experiences are predominant in your mind moment to moment, including any of your senses (hearing, touch, sight), thinking, or feeling. This creates a sense of distance (more on this technique later in the book).
- **Loving-kindness:** The practice of sending kind, caring thoughts to people, including yourself, and feeling that sense of warmth in your body. Being gentle and kind with ourselves takes so much of the sting of anxiety away. Often, our anxious thoughts have a punitive or self-critical attitude. What happens instead when we forgive ourselves and hold ourselves with care rather than irritation, fear, or judgment?

Every time you use any of the mindfulness techniques from above, you are teaching your brain to be different in the face of old triggers. You are giving yourself a chance to feel something new, to react differently, and to tread some new neural pathways. With anxiety, our minds are hyper-focused on the negative and the threatening. But being mindful tunes us into the positive. You may be surprised to find that breathing, slowing down, and being kind to yourself actually feels pretty good. In time, you may even prefer this to your ordinary sense of "relief" that avoidance used to give you!

Annie has made her arrangement with her accountability partner and has worked hard to change the cues and rewards of a certain behavior. This will take her far. But in the moment-to-moment unfolding of her experience, she can continually remind herself to be mindful and aware of what is happening. This is a very different state of mind to the fearful hyperfocus we get in a runaway anxiety loop. This is the feeling we get when we consciously stop, look around us, and become cognizant of what is happening. From that point, we have a choice to behave differently.

So Annie is on the treadmill one day, and despite being near the AC, she notices that she is beginning to feel hot. She recognizes that awful sinking feeling of panic rising in her—slow at first and then all at once it seems to be there. *It's happening again . . .* she thinks. But this time, instead of strapping herself in for the anxiety rollercoaster her body has done so many times before, she deliberately pauses and becomes mindful.

She immediately checks in with herself. With gentle and kind awareness, she notices those familiar feelings across her skin and the speed at which her thoughts are beginning to run. She sees all this and decides there and then to change her thoughts. She tells herself, "I am experiencing these sensations, but I don't have to react to them. I am not in any danger. I recognize this old anxiety loop because I've been here before, and I've come out of it. I'm okay. I'm learning new ways to cope. What do I want to do right now?"

She looks down at the clock on the treadmill dashboard and, regulating her breathing, tells herself to just focus on the number changing, one second reliably after the other. She reminds herself that they are just sensations. She thinks of how she ran on the treadmill yesterday with no problem, and she can do it again today. It's difficult. Several times she feels herself being pulled again into that same old panic spiral. Several times she pulls herself back. But something interesting happens—she is still on the treadmill when she notices that the feeling is starting to subside. Eventually it passes completely. For today, Annie has broken the cycle and taken a step toward something new and better.

A word of warning here: analyzing and unpicking the components of your own stress response is a fantastic skill to learn. But don't make it a purely intellectual exercise. Overthinkers and worriers tend to be rather good at ruminating endlessly and examining a tiny detail from multiple angles. This is **not** what you're doing when you familiarize yourself with the anxiety loop, however. Done incorrectly, analyzing and unpicking can just make anxiety worse. So how do you know the difference? Well, ask yourself to take every insight and understanding and *convert it to real change using action*. Don't just learn something new about yourself and think "huh, that's interesting." Ask what small change you can make right now. Then watch what happens. Unless your analyzing and unpicking results in concrete changes in your world, it will serve no purpose.

Chapter 3: Change Your Soundtrack

Jon Acuff is the author of the bestseller *Soundtracks*, and he would agree. According to him,

> **"The antidote to overthinking isn't more thinking—the antidote is action**. You don't think your way out of overthinking. You act your way out. You retire broken soundtracks. You replace them with new ones. You repeat them so often they become as automatic as the old ones. Those are all actions."

What does he mean by "soundtracks"? Well, it's exactly what it sounds like. Acuff thinks all of us have our own inner mental commentary that's always running in the background of our life, like the soundtrack of a movie. Have you ever noticed how the feel of a movie scene can completely change depending on whether its neutral scenes are accompanied by a laugh track, silence, or scary horror movie music? It's the same, says Acuff, with life. His goal, then, is to help people challenge undermining soundtracks and create new, supportive ones.

According to Acuff, it isn't a problem to occasionally have negative thoughts. The problem is that we *believe* everything we think. Later in the book, we'll look at the power of gaining distance from your thoughts and perceptions and not simply taking everything you experience as plain fact. The first step for now, however, is to start paying attention to your soundtrack and noticing what it does for you. Then, become curious about what it would look like to do something else.

Here's an example to show just what a difference "soundtracks" can make. Imagine a movie scene where the main character picks up their mail, only to discover a speeding fine. They pause and look at the letter, then open it to see that it'll cost them two hundred dollars. Now, picture this same scene but occurring in different movies. In movie one, there is no music, the person looks at the fine, sighs, and puts it on their desk to deal with later. In movie two, there is a low thumping noise that gradually gets louder and louder, ending with some screeching *Psycho*-style violins. In movie three, there is some gentle comedic music, with trumpets and a playful upbeat tempo.

Can you see how the music choice completely changes the meaning of the scene? Now imagine that instead of a musical soundtrack, you have a mental one.

Movie one: the person tells themselves, "Oh man, that's annoying, but never mind. I'll deal with it when I get home later."

Movie two: the person tells themselves, "Yup, typical. No wonder you can't get anywhere in life, with the way you keep burning money. You were an idiot and now you're going to be short this month. And you can bet that it's going to be a pain to try to pay this thing. You know what they're like. What's next? These things always come in threes, so watch out. That stupid car's engine is due to start giving me trouble any day now, I can just feel it . . . typical! But then again, why worry about two hundred dollars, right? You were never going to get a chance to save money, anyway, fine or no fine..."

Movie three: the person tells themselves, "Oops! A fine! Well, such is life. What are you gonna do? It's only two hundred dollars."

Remember, though, that in every scene, the events are *precisely the same*. The soundtrack, though, can turn neutral events into a drama, a comedy, or a horror. Any time you overthink or give in to anxiety, it's like dialing up that creepy horror-movie music. You know that your soundtrack is a problem if it is getting in the way of what you want—whether that's peace of mind, self-esteem, productivity, or better relationships. Once you identify an unhelpful soundtrack (which is basically the same as repetitive negative self-talk), then you can consciously replace it with one that works for you. And the way to do that? With action.

Tip 1: Ask if your thoughts are true, kind, or helpful

Not all thoughts are created equal.
Not everything you think is an accurate reflection of reality.
Not every thought is in your best interest.

The first step to stopping overthinking is to figure out which thoughts are making you feel bad and get rid of them. You can identify bad soundtracks by asking:

- Is this true?
- Is this helpful?
- Is this kind?

Only thoughts that pass all three criteria get to earn a space in your head!

Let's look at the example of opening a speeding fine in the mail. You might have the thought "Gah! Life is just so impossible!" Okay, fine. Pause and look at it. It's a natural, totally valid response (we've probably all had this thought at one point or another). But do we really want this kind of thought to expand and take over as the dominant soundtrack to our lives? Probably not.

Is it true? Not really. It's a bit dramatic. Life definitely is hard at times, sometimes very hard, but it's not impossible—at least not just because of a speeding fine.

Is it helpful? Well, not at all. It doesn't make it easier for you to find a solution, it doesn't inspire hope or creativity, it's not funny, it doesn't improve your relationships, and it does precisely nothing to help anyone get to any goal they have.

Is it kind? Not especially. In fact, in a way, it is unkind to assume that you are completely incapable of managing life. Bit of an insult when you think about it!

So, this thought fails to meet the standard, and fails hard. But you might have another anxiety-provoking thought, such as: "Speeding is idiotic. You deserve the fine; you could have killed someone!" This thought is kind of true, and it is helpful in the sense that it will probably get you to reduce your speed and be a more mindful driver. But it's definitely not kind! You could achieve the same effect by thinking "I was driving faster than I realized, and I know that that can be dangerous. Going forward, I'm going to make an effort to be more aware of my speed."

Here's another test you can pass any soundtrack through to see if it's a good one: Mentally repeat the same words to the person you love most in the world, or imagine yourself saying the same thing to an innocent four-year-old. This will quickly highlight any distortions you might have been happy to subject yourself to!

Tip 2: Flip the soundtrack

The good news is that when you find a negative thought, you can turn it around and use it against itself. One of the best places to do this is when you say things like "I must" or "It has to be perfect" or "I have to finish the whole thing right now."

Once you find these negative noises, just decide to play the opposite over and over to cultivate a completely different frame of mind.

"I'll never save any money" becomes "Even if it's just a few dollars here and there, I *can* save money if I try."

"The car engine might break" becomes "The car engine might not break."

"You always mess things up" becomes "You sometimes do things right."

You don't have to change the literal facts of your life; you just have to decide that you're not going to constantly play negative music over it!

Tip 3: Borrow soundtracks from those you admire

Other people are another great way to find new music to listen to. For example, Kanye West once said, "My life is dope and I do dope sh*t!" Acuff himself used this one to start seeing his life in a completely different way. If you listen carefully, you may hear snippets of other people's soundtracks. How does it feel to think like they do?

Maybe one day you hear someone remark, "Other people's opinions are not part of my decision-making on this." It strikes you as completely bold, self-assured, and powerful. It turns out, that is one possible soundtrack you could play! You might try it on yourself the next time you're stressing and being a people-pleaser. You repeat the line to yourself in your head and notice the shift in your attitude—and anxiety levels.

You can borrow soundtracks from anywhere whenever you want. You could add to your new "thought playlist" anything that makes you feel good, or is helpful, kind, and true. This is the real power about learning to master your soundtrack—*you* become the DJ presiding over it all, *you* are the movie director, and *you* can decide how you are going to narrate your own life to yourself.

Tip 4: Embed your new soundtracks into an item to make them permanent

Remember that action makes the difference. A key lesson from Acuff is to always have something with you that serves as a reminder of your favorite "soundtracks." Yes, an actual physical item you can carry in your pocket.

To make a positive thought stick, you can pick up an object and use it as a symbol for that positive thought. For example, if you had a good vacation with your family at the beach and you loved the soundtrack you played for those moments, you can pick up a rock at that beach to help you remember that relaxed, in-control state of mind. The next time you're stuck overthinking, all you have to do is grab hold of that rock and remind yourself that you can change the soundtrack.

Learning to Emotionally Recalibrate

If your life was a movie, what genre would it be? Would it be a heart-warming, feel-good romantic comedy? A bleak documentary that makes you want to slit your wrists? A goofy comedy that comes with a hidden message of hope? And in this movie, what character are you playing? The victim, villain, savior, or misunderstood genius? The helpful doormat? The doomed lover?

The good thing about being honest about the ruts we get stuck in is that we also give ourselves permission to be something else—remember that all of this is just habit. And it can be changed. If you have starred as the tortured victim of a nail-biting thriller for as long as you can remember, it will take time to rewrite the script. But you can. In previous chapters, we've considered that the anxiety response is both a **mental** and a **physiological** response. But it's also an **emotional** one. Learning to let go of anxiety is a question of changing how you *feel* about your life, not just the cognitive stories you tell or the physical symptoms you experience.

For many anxious people, the deeper emotion behind their worry and overthinking is extremely negative. It's about:

Low self-worth

Fear

Resentment

Insecurity

Guilt and shame

Overwhelm and exhaustion

Sadness

. . . and many more. So when we say "I'm anxious," it could be concealing a whole tapestry of different emotional threads, which include, "I feel unconfident in my abilities" or "I feel like I can't trust others to look out for me." When we talk about changing soundtracks, then, it's also about changing how we actually *feel*—not just the words we are saying to ourselves mentally. If you say "you've got this; you'll be okay," but you still feel completely overwhelmed and terrified, you haven't changed the soundtrack at all. Perhaps you've kept the same song and just called it something different!

Here's an exercise to try. Off the top of your head, think of two goals that you would like to achieve in life but haven't yet. It doesn't matter if it's a big or small one. Now, look at this goal and carefully notice how it makes you feel to read it. Notice what instantly pops into your mind when you read—for example, "complete a marathon." Listen to the words you use when you speak to yourself, but also how it feels. Become familiar with the fear, self-doubt, whatever. Then try to invert this emotional soundtrack, too. What would it feel like to be excited, curious, or confident instead?

Let's say Adam is training for a marathon, but he is sixty-seven years old, has a bad knee, and has never exercised in his life. It's a challenge, no doubt. His soundtrack is *not* the one from the Rocky movies. It's all doom and gloom: "I can't do this. I'm too old. Why did I sign up for this? This was a stupid idea."

But Adam stops and notices all this. He reminds himself that this constant running commentary is not a 100 percent accurate reflection of reality—it's just noises his brain is making at him. That's all. Literally just electrochemical energy in his brain, and nothing else. Once he can see this (versus just listening to it and taking it as gospel), he can start to challenge and question it. He likes to imagine, going on Acuff's advice, that he has a "pocket jury" that he passes these thoughts over to, and they decide whether the thoughts are true, helpful, and kind.

He runs these thoughts one by one through the jury, who all decide that he is being way, way too hard on himself. But he also notices the feeling behind all these thoughts. It's "anxiety," yes, but the more Adam gets curious about it, the more he sees that what he is feeling is apprehension—he wants to hope and strive for a big goal, but part of him is unsure because he doesn't know whether he is asking for a bitter disappointment, or worse, embarrassment, when those who support him find out he was a loser all along! Just as he notices the thoughts pop up, he detects this queasy feeling that comes with it.

How would he like to feel instead? He set the marathon goal in the first place because he wanted to feel strong, proud, and exhilarated. So he reminds himself of that. The next time he's lacing up his running shoes and feeling that soundtrack start to play, he pauses and reminds himself of a time when he felt strong and proud instead. He takes a few deep breaths and tries to conjure that feeling there and then. It's almost like this memory becomes a figurative beach stone from a vacation that he can pull from his pocket and hold in his hand. And in just the same way that you don't have to believe everything your brain tells you, you don't have to feel every emotion that pops up its head and demands your attention. Adam can choose instead to realize that the difficulty of a marathon is precisely the thing that is going to make him feel proud and strong at the end.

Acuff says,

> "People think a thought is just something that shows up on its own and you have no power. But once you say to yourself *I have the permission and the ability to choose what I think during the day, to choose the actions I will take,*

that's where it becomes really fun."

Summary:

- The more anxious you feel, the more afraid you are of that experience, and the more you try to avoid it—but this prevents you from learning about how anxiety operates, and therefore gaining power over it.
- Anxiety follows a familiar path: 1. Something internal or external triggers a fight-or-flight response, 2. Your brain adapts by finding ways to avoid that stimulus (rightly or wrongly), 3. The reward of temporary relief that reinforces the avoidance mechanism, 4. The inevitable return of heightened anxiety. Familiarity with this cycle allow you to check your response and intervene. Try a body scan and reflect on your process.
- Typically, we respond to our *thoughts about a trigger* and not strictly the trigger itself. Reverse the cycle by confronting feared situations without the help of unhealthy coping

mechanisms, then trying healthier alternatives.

- Anxiety is a learned behavior entrenched in habit. Our habit cycles are made of a triggering cue, the behavior itself, and a reward that reinforces it. Slow down and note what your cues and rewards are.
- Understand your anxiety habits and work with your brain rather than against it, replacing bad habits with better ones. Maintain an attitude of curiosity and compassion, and try to replace negative "soundtracks" with more positive or neutral ones.
- Ask if your soundtracks are kind, true, or helpful, and if not, invert them, or take inspiration from the soundtracks of people you admire. Tell yourself: *I have the permission and the ability to choose what I think during the day and to choose the actions I will take.*

Part Two: Unraveling the Anxiety Response

Chapter 4: The Anxiety Timeline

Recall that the fight-or-flight response is one that necessarily *narrows perception*. When you are anxious or fearful, your attention will zoom right in on the one thing you are perceiving as a threat, and probably amplify it in the process. What this means is that being anxious is the opposite of being able to see the "bigger picture." And that can be a problem.

Using timelines is a way to gain that broader perspective again and reacquaint yourself with the bigger picture that anxiety can sometimes cause you to lose sight of. Here's a question that may seem strange to you: How do you know that what you're experiencing is actually anxiety?

The truth is that what many of us interpret as anxiety is actually a complicated cocktail of so-called "meta-emotions" that completely overwhelm us and make it difficult to identify with any clarity. When you are trapped in an anxiety spiral, all you know is that it feels bad and you want it to stop. But you lose any sense of what is happening and why, and you may also lose all sense of proportion.

Timelining can be an antidote for this. It will help you break down the big, confusing mess that anxiety can be into smaller, more manageable pieces. It will help you put those pieces into a logical order and link them up with a narrative that helps you contextualize what's actually happening. Now, timeline exercises usually cannot be done right when you're experiencing a peak of anxiety or worry. No matter how strong your willpower, things are simply moving too fast for you to make sense of them. Ever feel like your head is rushing a million miles an hour? That's not a time to embark on a timeline exercise!

Instead, do this exercise as a kind of "anxiety post-mortem" when you're feeling a little calmer. Looking from the outside, you are able to see the event with more neutral eyes and move through the memory almost as though you have a pause, rewind, and fast forward button and you're watching it as a film.

Pause: stop for a moment and remember a particular episode, really focusing on what happened and what you felt and thought. Knowing your anxiety symptoms and triggers can help you identify future anxiety episodes. These sensations then stop serving as triggers but instead become little alerts that bring you to awareness and give you the opportunity to run a different program.

Rewind: this helps you see what may have contributed to your anxiety in the situation. Were you "going down rabbit holes" online? Drinking too much coffee? Dwelling again on that embarrassing memory from five years ago?

Fast forward: zoom ahead to the outcome of the situation and look at your responses to your anxiety. Did you get anxious because you were anxious? Did you berate yourself, apologize, feel shame? Look at this consequence clearly and see it now, without judgment.

Do the timeline exercise with a pen and paper, or else using a word processor. Take your time and reconstruct the event as best as you can, almost like you're a forensic detective piecing together a crime. Put things in chronological order and look for connects and cause-and-effect relationships. Look for cues and triggers, look for rewards and reinforcers, look for automatic thoughts and feelings. Be curious about how the difficult episode came to a close. What helped? What didn't?

What you are trying to do is figure out how you have interpreted the event and the meanings you have ascribed to certain points in the timeline. What begins as a stressful, confusing muddle can start to look like a clearer picture. You can construct timelines to dissect particularly intense moments, like a panic attack, or you could take a long view and use a timeline to explore a whole year, or more.

In the context of therapy, timeline exercises can help bring to light pivotal but often-overlooked personal experience. Sometimes, you need to see everything all together on one page to have that lightbulb moment. As usual, this works best if you replace judgment and assumption with compassion and genuine curiosity. Don't let your "soundtrack" or inner critic jump in too quickly to tell you the same old story. Instead, look at it as though for the first time. Look for patterns. Look for something beneath the surface.

Let's see how we can apply the above to an example.

Lydia is making a big presentation at work, and as D-day approaches, she starts to notice she is feeling pretty anxious. On the day, she feels unsure of herself, bungles some of the delivery, and receives a few critical remarks from her boss. Now she is home after work and trying to process what happened. She sits down to explore.

Pause: Let's look at the details. At the time she was sweating and felt her heart pounding, she had a weird tight feeling in her stomach, and there was a lot of tension in her neck and shoulders. She took some deep breaths and soldiered on with the presentation, but still felt anxious.

Rewind: Lydia thinks carefully about what may have triggered her anxiety, and realizes that she only got anxious after learning that there would be someone from another branch sitting in on the presentation. She writes down all the thoughts she had at that moment. "An outsider will instantly see how stupid my ideas are." She also writes down all the emotions she recalls feeling: exposed, vulnerable, foolish, small, unconfident. She also noticed that there was a secondary reaction—i.e., she felt stupid about feeling stupid! There were other triggers too. She recalls staying up late the night before and skipping breakfast that morning, instead opting for more coffee than she usually had to pep her up. She is beginning to see some cause and effect.

Fast forward: After receiving some feedback from her boss, she recalls going into a mini meltdown and immediately getting defensive. On the drive home, she noticed herself ruminating over his words, seemingly making them worse and worse each time until she felt sick with anxiety.

After calming down, though, she can see that she actually missed all the good points—the positive feedback and the fact that she completed her presentation despite feeling anxious.

Once all this has been written, Lydia takes a piece of paper and literally draws a timeline from left to write. She plots all the events, starting from the previous night, and ends a few hours after the presentation. She draws a line to show where her anxiety rose and fell. Simply doing this calms her down and gives her a sense of perspective, but the real work comes when she starts to ask questions:

- How might she respond to these triggers differently in the future, knowing what she knows now?
- What helped reduce anxiety in the moment, and what made it worse?
- What was the main trigger?
- Can she see any factors that were staining and maintaining the anxiety?
- What did she think and feel, and can she put a more positive spin on it now that she's calmer?

- If she could go back to certain points in the timeline now, what would she tell herself?

Lydia might then decide to close her eyes and visualize the entire scenario again, but this time change it. She might picture different choices she might make, and different ways she might respond to triggers. She might rehearse an alternative ending to the story and add in a breathing exercise or affirmation to help soothe her nerves.

When the exercise is completely finished, Lydia realizes something: Her boss had a point. Once she can dial down her anxiety, she can see his feedback more clearly and realize that he was actually helping her and that his notes could be extremely useful going forward. But this is not something she could have processed if she had left her anxious experiences in a knot and decided not to unravel them further.

To follow the process Lydia did, try the following:

1. First just describe the event in as neutral terms as possible. Note your feelings, your thoughts, your bodily

sensations, and your actions. Describe what was happening around you.
2. Look to what happened immediately before and be curious about triggers and contributing factors (remember that a trigger can be purely internal, such as a memory).
3. What happened after the main anxiety event? Note what you did, your emotions, and how effective your coping strategies were. What meaning did you ascribe to certain events or sensations?
4. Continue to explore the event, perhaps even replaying it while rehearsing a different ending. What have you learned?

If the above seems long-winded, rest assured that this kind of unraveling doesn't need to take a long time. But it does need a moment of conscious reflection, a little honesty, and a lot of compassion. Don't assume that your first interpretation of any stressful event is the most accurate one. You may find that this technique almost always makes events seem a lot less catastrophic than they seemed at first!

Long-Term Anxiety Patterns

The timeline tool is not just useful for dissecting bad days at the office. **It can help you gain an even broader sense of bigger overarching patterns**—for example, why you tend to gravitate toward jobs that aren't right for you, why you usually quit after three or four years, and why the same story seems to be playing out every time this pattern repeats.

Try the following exercise when you have twenty minutes to spare:

Take an A4 piece of paper, landscape orientation, and a pen, and draw a long line from left to right to represent your entire life (so far). The very leftmost part is your birth, and the right is present day. Divide the line up evenly so that every year or decade is shown in its correct proportion to the rest of the line. This line represents chronological time. Next, you are going to draw two more lines: One that represents your overall state of mind, and the other tracks your most significant life events.

For the first line, try to think back over each year of your life and, using the y-axis (the vertical left edge of the paper), mark how you felt on, say, a ten-point scale. You could show your mood as neutral (zero), perfect and blissful (ten points above neutral), or the worst you've ever felt (ten points below). While you're drawing this up-and-down line, you can simultaneously draw in the other line that shows the main events happening at the time. A main event can be a big thing like the birth of a child, the loss of a job, emigrating, winning the lottery, or getting married, but you get to decide what is significant—if there is a single poignant memory that you feel was pivotal in your life, include it, even though it may seem small to others.

Let's say Lydia does this exercise in addition to the shorter timeline exercise above. She marks on her graph all the big events: every new job, every relationship start to end, all the big house moves, health disasters, and life-changing holidays. You can see where this is going: When Lydia looks at everything on one page, she may start to see patterns that were kind of hidden before.

She might notice that, almost like clockwork, her anxiety tends to skyrocket in the few months after starting a new job. She may notice that her worst years were always those in which she moved houses, and that she tended to be happier when she was in a relationship than when she was single. Some insights might be truly surprising—for example, she *thought* that changing jobs or being fired was the worst thing that could happen, but when she actually looks at the timeline, these periods in her life were in fact marked by a feeling of *relief*. The most stressful moments are, she realizes, the times when she begins a new job.

Doing this exercise for the longer term has many benefits. **It gives you the bigger picture and lets you challenge certain assumptions that many not be correct. Remember that anxiety is just a story we're telling ourselves, and it may be accurate or it may not be.** This is true for the bigger overarching stories we let anxiety tell us. For example, we may have a story that goes, "Because I'm not as smart as other people, I find things more difficult, and that's why I've never really progressed in my career." But then you construct the timeline, and you see a different story. You *have* progressed in your career. Maybe it's time to throw the old story out!

Naturally, this exercise is limited by the accuracy of your own memory—of course, you could just project your own distortions and biases onto it. But it works best if you can be as honest as possible. If you have someone you trust, ask them to look over your graph; you may be surprised at what they agree and disagree with. As you complete it, ask the following questions to get a richer sense of the way anxiety has played a role in your life:

Overall, what has proceeded your most anxious periods in life?
Overall, what allowed you to overcome those periods? What made things better?
Is there any main theme that seems to recur across your timeline? What big idea is connecting all the separate events?
How do you look at past events now, and how does this compare to what you felt about them as they happened?
If you struggle with anxiety, can you pinpoint the moment when it started? What else was happening then?
Is there an overarching story that you've been telling about your anxiety, which links all these events together?

Chapter 5: The ABCDE Method

Albert Ellis, the so-called "grandfather of cognitive behavioral therapy" noticed something interesting about the patients who would visit him. He saw that **different people would have entirely different reactions to the same events.** This observation was not new even then—the Stoic philosopher noted that, "you are disturbed not by things, but the views which you take of them." This means that when you sit down and try to tackle the problem of anxiety, a good starting point may not be the things that you believe are stressing you out, but your reaction to those things—the stress itself.

For Ellis, the heart of the matter was our set of beliefs about the world. He was one of the first to lay out a framework of triggers and rewards that came before and after such beliefs:

A—Activating event
B—Belief
C—Consequence

In true Stoic fashion, the activating event is neutral—it has no intrinsic meaning of its own. But our brain responds to it in a particular way, and that results in B, our belief. Ellis believed that there were broadly two types of belief: rational and irrational. So, the activating event might be a black cat walking on the road in front of you. An irrational belief may be "I'm going to have a bad day now," and a rational belief may be "Oh, there's a cat. Cute."

According to Ellis, the former response will lead to largely negative consequences, C, while the latter will lead to largely positive ones (here, "rational" is not quite meant in a philosophical sense, but more along the lines of what we already covered—beliefs that are accurate, useful, and kind). The logic goes that if you can see that you are experiencing negative emotions (let's say, overthinking and anxiety), then somewhere along the line, you have entertained an irrational or unhelpful thought.

In the late 80s' British sitcom *Red Dwarf*, there is a storyline involving a character who gets to see how his life might have played out in an alternate universe. The two lives branch off at a single pivotal point: whether the character gets held back in school for a year or not. One life turns out to be heroic and successful, and the other turns out to be (comically) awful. Throughout this episode, the viewer is assuming that the character with the awful life was the one who was held back. He bemoans his fate and blames this limiting incident for setting his life on the wrong course forever. He claims that the other possible life, the one that turned out brilliantly, only worked out that way because that version of the character was allowed to advance a grade, unlike him.

The twist at the end of the episode, however, reveals that it was in fact the uber-successful version of the character that was held back, and not the other way around. This ultra-successful version explains that this event was really the single best thing that happened to him. It allowed him to grow, to learn more about himself, to rise to the challenge, and so on. The other, less successful version, became that way because he was never so challenged. We see that this event (being held back or not held back) is actually neutral, and that what has really determined the two characters' fates is their *response* to the event, and not the event itself.

You don't need a parallel-universe plot device to see this same thing play out all the time in real life. For example, imagine that a young author named Stephen King submits a manuscript and it gets rejected. He thinks to himself, "Well, I'll just keep submitting it until someone says yes. I don't care how long that takes." He submits the manuscript a total of thirty times to publishers, and it is rejected every time, eventually getting accepted (incidentally, this is actually true).

Meanwhile, a similarly talented author Stephanie Queen submits a manuscript, and it, too, gets rejected. She thinks, "Well, that's proof that the whole idea was stupid. I should quit now before I embarrass myself further." Her manuscript never gets to be rejected thirty times because she never submits it anywhere again.

Both authors possess the same talent and experienced the same event (rejection). But their entire lives went on different paths because of the wildly different beliefs they had about what this event meant. This is what Ellis meant when he said that an irrational belief is one that leads to negative consequences. At the time, Stephanie Queen may well have believed that a cautious, cynical attitude was "rational." But seeing the bigger view and the broader consequences, we probably have a different conclusion.

The Real Way to Use CBT for Anxiety

Too many people have been taught a version of CBT (cognitive behavioral therapy) that is very limited and simplistic. They learn about the ABC model and assume that it refers to events and beliefs on a small scale, like a ringing bell eliciting a salivation response in Pavlov's dogs. It's no surprise, then, that they find the model quite impractical when it comes to applying it to their real, complex lives.

You may encounter examples of how someone is nervous to speak in public, and so they examine the belief that makes them feel this way ("everyone thinks I'm stupid"), change it, and presto, their fear of public speaking disappears. You probably know by now that it is seldom as straightforward as this!

That's because our beliefs are not just momentary thoughts we have in discrete situations. Rather, as previous chapters have shown, they are woven right through the fabric of our entire lives. They inform how we think, how we feel, our sense of identity, how we make meaning, and the way we act. CBT will be a shallow solution so long as it only deals with the superficial manifestations of our beliefs. In other words, you are not a machine, and it's not possible to simply go into your programming and change every "I'm stupid" to "I'm not stupid" and then press play.

Truly transforming your negative and limiting beliefs is deep, difficult work. But it's the best work you will ever do. Before we move on and look at how to do this in a meaningful way, we should explore one important caveat: Sometimes, your beliefs are not the problem.

Before you embark on a program of self-CBT, thoroughly examine your environment and make sure that it is not the real cause behind your current mental state. If you are in an abusive relationship (that includes work!) or if you are living in a toxic, unsafe, or undermining environment, then your first task is to get out of that environment. There is no point in adjusting your mental processes so that you can better adapt to an unhealthy environment!

No amount of CBT will cancel out your anxiety if that anxiety is a healthy and "rational" response to a poor environment. If you're dealing with deep grief or feel like you're wrestling some heavy existential questions, CBT likely won't help. But you can take the Stoic's lead on this, too: Have the serenity to accept what you can't change, the courage to change what you can't accept, and the wisdom to know the difference.

If something in your life is creating or sustaining anxiety, do what you can to remove it. If it cannot be removed, try to accept it as best you can and mitigate its effects with stress management techniques (we'll explore these later). This should help you tease out what portion of the problem is your own unhealthy thought process. And this is where CBT is best applied.

Challenging Your Beliefs

The ABC model is descriptive. It shows us how our beliefs operate. **By adding two extra letters, though, we extend the model and create a framework for conscious change.** The extra letters are:

D—Disputation
E—Effect

Disputation is the simple act of challenging and questioning the belief, B. it's a way to change the consequence by disrupting the narrative that created it. Let's say the author Stephanie Queen decided to address her negative thought patterns, particularly this one:

"Well, that's proof that the whole idea was stupid. I should quit now before I embarrass myself further."

This belief, she realizes, has cropped up over and over in her life:

"Failure is humiliating."

"If I don't know how to do something first time round, then I have no talent for it and may as well give up."
"People disliking my work means I'm a bad person."
"It's embarrassing to create bad art."

All of these beliefs lead to a very reliable consequence: she feels defeated, demotivated, ashamed, and disheartened. And this in turn affects her behavior and choices. If she has told herself that putting her work out there and getting rejected is the worst thing that can happen, naturally she won't keep doing that. Maybe she stops writing entirely. Ten years later, she tells people, "I wanted to be an author once, but I wasn't cut out for it." The belief has altered how she interprets reality and how she thinks of her identity. Can you see how the belief has infiltrated *everything*? And yet, what happened to her was identical to what happened to Stephen King.

Challenging these beliefs is not simply a matter of inverting them. Remember that anxiety and overthinking come with an emotional component, too. So, gradually, Stephanie Queen works on her overall attitude. Is it really true that failure is the end of the world? Isn't it a necessary part of learning and growing? She gently challenges her assumptions. Does she really think that people who are not instant experts are unworthy of trying again so they can learn? She might discover that no, she only seems to hold herself to this bizarre standard. She challenges herself to look at the early work of famous artists. Were they brilliant from the start? No. They had to "fail" a little first to learn and get better.

Gradually, she chips away at these negative assumptions and replaces them with something that is gentler, more reasonable, more useful. And this is where we get to E, the effect. This is the new consequence we create when we change our beliefs. Let's say Stephanie tries something completely different. She does a little experiment and joins a writing group. She challenges herself to share work with other writers before it's perfect. She gets feedback, not all of it positive, and observes that it really isn't the end of the world to realize that something could have been done better. In fact, after doing this for some months, she realizes that she has started to relish and seek out critical feedback precisely because it is making her a better writer.

Here we see another important aspect of well-applied CBT: **It is always better to cement new beliefs with action**. You never need to just believe something different for no reason. If you don't *really* believe that "failure is just part of the process," then the only thing that will change your mind is literally having an experience that proves this belief untrue. Stephanie takes baby steps where she creates the opportunity for a different experience. She gets rejected and notices that she doesn't fall over and die. In fact, she sees how little it really matters. She develops not only resilience, but gradually changes the assumptions on which her entire life is running.

Stephen King is famous for saying how he took every rejection letter he received from a publisher and hung it proudly on his study wall, where he could see it as he wrote. For him, failure wasn't the end of the world, but a dare and a powerful motivation to keep going.

Try to apply the principles of CBT to your own life in the same way. Going beyond the superficial will take time and honesty. But you can begin by simply asking some questions:

- What are the main events that have occurred in my life?
- How have I interpreted these events? What stories have I told about them? How have they informed my beliefs?
- What emotions have those beliefs caused for me?
- What actions (or inactions) have resulted?
- Are my beliefs helping me achieve the kind of life I really want?
- Looking at my life, is there an alternative way I could have interpreted everything?
- If I adopted this alternative view, how would I behave? How would I feel?

DON'T "Fake It Till You Make It"

When it comes to anxiety, overthinking, panic, or worry, there is seldom a quick fix. You may find that your anxiety has deep roots and is held in place by a lifetime's worth of habits, beliefs, and assumptions. By now, it's probably becoming clear to you why cheesy "affirmations" are so seldom effective. If you don't *genuinely believe* them, then they are worthless. You'll only create cognitive dissonance and even worsen the problem by alienating yourself from what you actually feel.

Instead of trying to fake it till you make it, take action. Challenge your beliefs and put them out in the real world to test them. If you have the belief "I can't do it because people will laugh at me," then don't just sit quietly in a room and try to argue yourself out of the belief. Instead, get out into the world and prove to yourself that it's not true. Take a tiny, tiny risk. Do it and notice that people don't laugh at you. Or, perhaps they *do* laugh at you—and it's not nearly as bad as you thought! The best argument against fear and anxiety is to take action that proves to you your own competence and builds up evidence for what is real. Take a small step, then take another. At the heart of much anxiety is the thought "I can't cope with this." So teach yourself that you *can* cope by setting up a series of small challenges where you show yourself that you are more than capable.

Chapter 6: Managing Expectations

Ellie has just had a baby. It has been something she has wanted for a long time and planned for many years. She is completely committed to doing the very best she can and has taken every class and read every parenting book within months of finding out she was pregnant. One day, her weeks-old infant screams all through the night and has a raging fever in the morning. Ellie is exhausted, terrified, and eaten up with guilt: What has she done wrong? She is stunned to find herself feeling resentful of the baby, angry at the doctors and nurses, and just about ready to divorce her husband.

Within three days, she is a ball of anxiety, and her thoughts are racing to some dark places. "I'm an awful mother. I'm failing. I've damaged my child forever. I've messed everything up." Later in the week, Ellie's mother comes over to help. She says to Ellie, "What's the big deal? Your kid had a fever. Kids get fevers every two minutes when they're little."

What's happened here? What is the cause of Ellie's anxiety?

If we look closely at Ellie's underlying beliefs about her situation, we might find one very pesky and very revealing word: SHOULD.

"He should not be this sick."
"I shouldn't be so upset by such a small problem."
"I should know how to deal with this."
"I should have put his beanie on yesterday."
"He shouldn't be crying."
"I shouldn't feel like I want to throw him out the window . . . that's *really* bad."

Reality is what actually occurs.
Expectations are demands we make on reality.

It would be ideal if these two were in sync, but in practice, they seldom are. Anxiety can be seen as growing in that distance between expectation and reality. When things don't go as planned, it's easy to feel let down, disappointed, and anxious. An expectation can feel like a rule that has been broken. Our belief can frame an unmet expectation as a problem—when it never really was one.

It's normal to have expectations of the world, but the problem comes when our expectations are unrealistic or (there's that word again) irrational. If Ellie is honest with herself, she would see a few unconscious expectations that don't really make sense. Perhaps social media has convinced her that she should be finding motherhood easier than it realistically can be. Perhaps her overly high standards have made her judge her own reasonable behavior as lacking somehow. If she takes a step back, though, she might see what her mother does—it really is no big deal!

When your expectations outpace reality, it can also mean that you don't appreciate what you do have. This is why anxiety problems tend to go hand in hand with a serious lack of gratitude. All while Ellie is stressing about her child's fever, she is not appreciating any of the other blessings in her life—like her attentive and loving husband. It's wonderful to have aspirations and to imagine better things that *could* be. It's wonderful to hope for something better and to hold yourself to high standards. But these should inspire you; they should never be so unrealistic that they cause anxiety and unhappiness.

What Are Your Expectations?

Expectations can come from our life experiences, from authority figures or parents, from demands society places on us, or from the media. Some expectations are great since they encourage us to push ourselves and work hard. But some are unconscious, automatic, unhelpful, and actively getting in the way—like Ellie's. Sometimes we can only learn how unrealistic an expectation is by falling short of it and realizing what we had been unconsciously feeling entitled to.

Is your expectation respectful, fair, compassionate? Is it properly considered and thought out, honest, and practical? Is it something that can literally happen in reality? If not, then it's likely to be an expectation that causes you problems.

Awareness is key to breaking the expectations-reality cycle. Knowing your expectations helps. Knowing what you "should" expect is also smart. An anxious person will adjust themselves to fit the expectation (spoiler alert—even if they succeed, the expectation moves, and they put themselves on a nice anxiety treadmill). A better thing to do is to adjust the expectations instead.

As you are getting more familiar with your own anxiety patterns and habits, take a look at your beliefs and interpretations and ask if your "rules" are actually reasonable. Look for this word SHOULD and ask if it's really fair for you to have expected what you did. Turn things around: If you drop this expectation, what happens? Do you notice that you suddenly feel less anxious? That's a good sign that you need to let go of the **idea you have of reality** and start embracing **reality**.

Cultivating Healthier Expectations

Tip 1: Stop comparing

Be honest and ask if the people around you (and on social media) are inspiring role models or tools for your own misery. Comparison is a process that always produces negativity, because when you compare, there is always a loser. Comparison can only end with the feeling that something is lacking.

Be ruthless with yourself and refuse to engage in the kind of comparison that always makes you feel like a loser. It's okay to admire people and be inspired to be like them. But if comparisons leave you feeling worse instead of better, or like giving up instead of persisting, then you know you don't need comparisons in your life.

Remind yourself that everyone struggles. Remind yourself that there's no competition and no prize at the end of your life for being perfect. If you're caught in a comparison spiral, pull out of it by asking what your standards and values are. How can you beat *your* own personal best according to *your* own principles? That's what matters.

Tip 2: Have self-compassion

When you say, "I should have been better," you are discounting all the good you have done. Why not say "I did the best I could with what I had"? This doesn't mean you let yourself off the hook for bad behavior, but what it means is that you don't beat yourself up for nothing. It means you're on your own side. Ellie can say to herself, "I'm finding this difficult because I haven't done it before. But I love my child and I'm doing okay. I'm proud of myself for persevering."

Tip 3: Ask for help

Sometimes we cast ourselves in some heroic role where it is solely up to us to save the world and do it all perfectly first time. We can forget that we don't have to single-handedly do everything ourselves, and that it's okay—and perfectly normal—to ask for help. Ask others for advice, support, or assistance. If you're overwhelmed with stress, ask if you're laboring under the expectation that all the work falls to you. Can you delegate?

Sometimes anxious people have become addicted to the martyr role, are workaholics, or have notoriously poor boundaries. They may suffer in silence because they have an expectation that they should help others and never expect any help in return. If this is the source of some of your anxiety, that's good news—it means it's completely possible for you to shrug it off and do less!

Tip 4: Reconnect to your values

What really makes you happy? At the end of the day, what do you most value? By anchoring into these things, you can offset some of the feelings of disappointment that come from unmet expectations.

Expectations and Core Beliefs

Our expectations and core beliefs can be deeply entangled with one another. For example, if we believe that "money is the only thing that will make me happy," then one day when we win the lottery, we may be very surprised to discover we are not much happier than before. Our expectation of blissful happiness came from our belief, and when our reality falls short, we can experience a host of negative feelings.

Any time you have a vision of how the future will play out, or a set idea of what you believe you want or need from a situation, then you have an expectation. And this expectation can be distorted. People are notoriously bad at guessing what will make them happy or fulfilled. They may say with certainty what they want or need, but this expectation is then shattered when it hits reality. Perhaps one cause of Ellie's anxiety is the kind of sobering realization that motherhood is nothing like she expected. It's not that she thought the situation itself would be different, but rather that she expected to *feel* different about it. She anticipated being much happier, more sure of herself, and more in control. Her anxiety comes from realizing that she doesn't feel this way at all, in reality.

If you are anxious and ruminating over something, ask what these negative feelings are telling you about your expectations and the beliefs underlying them:

- What exactly did you expect to happen? Be clear and specific.
- Where did these expectations come from?
- Is the expectation realistic, helpful, and kind?
- If not, can you adjust it?
- Do you feel your anxiety and disappointment lessen if you abandon your expectations?

The Single Best Way to Rewrite Expectations . . .

Be grateful!

You've heard it all before, but practicing gratitude can make an enormous difference in your life. Reorient your attention to what is working. Keep perspective. When you consistently look at something and judge it as lacking, seeing only what it could or should be, you miss all the wonderful things it *is*. Get into the habit of regularly counting your blessings. And count your "problems" too—they are often not problems at all, but lessons and opportunities.

You've probably heard of suggestions like thinking of or writing down a few things you feel grateful for every day. While this is a good idea, let's be honest—how long will it be before you're just going through the motions? The truth is that these sorts of rote practices aren't the best way to genuinely create a shift in your brain chemistry. Again, it's not about identifying something to be grateful for on an intellectual level and understanding that cognitively. It's about conjuring up those sincere feelings of thankfulness.

Here are a few ideas to try, but keep in mind always that you are not merely checking something off a to-do list, but cultivating a particular emotional state of mind.

Don't just think about how grateful you are, express it. Literally say thank you to people or express out loud how happy you are for certain things. This will make it all the more concrete and real for you. It may also be a nice idea to create little family or social rituals around gratitude. Don't wait for Thanksgiving; every birthday or Christmas, or every evening at the dinner table, try sharing with friends or family what you are appreciative.

Gratitude can be powerful when you receive it, too, and not just give it. Keep a list of moments when others thanked you and appreciated you. Read back over these moments and remind yourself of that exact emotional experience, seeing what subtle changes it brings to your perspective.

The media you consume plays a big role in your life. **Be more discerning about the**

kinds of narratives and stories you are surrounding yourself with. "Gratitude narratives" are those that are inspiring and orient you toward appreciation and awareness of the good things in life. Be careful: A lot of so-called self-help is actually brimming with narratives that draw attention to lack, instead. Try to limit your intake of before-and-after-style transformations, which may reinforce the idea that your present reality is always an unfinished, unappreciated work in progress, and not something to be treasured and appreciated as it is right now.

Make your gratitude multi-sensorial. Being thankful is not just an abstract thing. When you think about it, pausing to really relish and savor pleasurable things in your environment is a way to show your gratitude. After all, how can you be thankful for something if you haven't even slowed down enough to become aware of its existence? You might go on a "savoring walk" where you nurture feelings of gratitude across all five senses. Feel the gorgeous warmth of the sunshine, look at the millions of different shades of green and brown, taste the coolness of the air, smell the soil underfoot, hear the wind—and be gently accepting and thankful for it all. Isn't it sufficient just as it is?

Finally, **get into the habit of emotional acceptance**. This concept will be very alien to some people, but if mastered can create dramatic changes in your mindset. It may be a major shift for you to even imagine that your emotional state is something to be grateful for—but it is!

Consider that people who experience anxiety tend to think of certain emotions as good and certain emotions as bad. Having a panic attack or being obsessive or over-worried are "bad"—and that means you want to avoid them. But rejecting your genuine experience this way can, surprise, surprise, create more negative emotions and more of the anxiety you're trying to avoid.

Gratitude and acceptance are close cousins. Being able to just see an emotional experience for what it is without trying to rush past it and go to the next thing—this is a powerful mindfulness technique that will take the sting out of anxiety. What happens to anxiety when you just let it be? What happens when you don't judge it, hate it, argue against it, run from it in terror, shame it, or try to interpret it? What happens when you don't see it and immediately start making a plan to be rid of it?

This approach comes from a therapeutic model called Acceptance and Commitment Therapy (or ACT), and it's all about learning to tolerate uncomfortable or intense emotions. Here's how to use the approach to gently get on top of anxiety.

Step 1: Identify your emotion. Give it a name. If there are more than two, name all of them. Use a symbol, metaphor, or description if that helps.

Step 2: Get some distance. Now that you have a name for it, put that name some place outside of yourself, with some breathing room between you and it. Close your eyes and imagine that the feeling is literally outside of you, a few feet away from your body. Get enough distance so that you can observe it without identifying with it.

Step 3: Give the feeling a shape. It has a name, but now become curious about its other characteristics. If the feeling were a size or a color or an animal, what would it be? If it were a movement or a flavor or a person, what would that look like? Then just watch it. You are learning to *recognize the feeling without reacting to it.*

Step 4: Reflect. At any point, you can bring that emotion back to yourself again and reflect on how the exercise felt. How did it feel? Did the intensity diminish with the distance? How do you feel before and after identifying and naming the feeling? Over time, and if you practice this exercise often enough, you will notice that your relationship to your emotions (even the strong ones) will start to change and mature.

When you are comfortable just observing, you get better at identifying and naming. And when you can name a thing and put your finger on it, you gain psychological distance from it. If you are not so closely entangled and identified with it, you start to realize something: that you are in charge of how you engage with it—if you engage at all. You also start to see that sometimes what you thought was a "bad emotion" was actually just neutral, or in some cases, it even has some value to you, if only you have enough presence of mind to accept and welcome how it feels.

Summary:

- The fight-or-flight response is one that *narrows perception*, but a timeline exercise can reacquaint you with the bigger picture. Look from the outside to see events with neutral eyes, and move through memories by pausing, rewinding, and fast forwarding to understand how it all comes together.
- Figure out how you have interpreted an event and the meanings you have ascribed to them, then become curious about healthier alternatives. This can also be done to identify long-term anxiety patterns across your whole life.
- "You are disturbed not by things, but the views which you take of them." The ABCDE model helps you identify the activating event, the belief, and the consequences of the belief, as well as identify the possibility of disputing the belief and observing the resulting effect. The method helps us identify our particular interpretations of neutral events and challenge our resulting beliefs about them. We cement new beliefs by applying them

and taking action—so *don't* fake it till you make it.
- The distance between reality and our unrealistic expectations can be a source of anxiety. Consider if your expectations are fair, rational, kind, and useful, and be aware of your idea of reality versus reality.
- Drop the word "should," stop comparing yourself to others, have compassion for yourself, ask for help, and reconnect to your values and principles rather than arbitrary and irrational expectations or standards. Be curious how your core beliefs are informing your expectations of how things should play out.
- Gratitude and emotional acceptance can help you embrace what is and encourage a healthier relationship to reality.

Part Three: Your Brain—Friend or Foe?

Chapter 7: Cognitive Distortions and the Triple Column Technique

The more you pause, become aware, and learn to accept your feelings while gaining some healthy distance from them, the more you will start to see patterns. Your "soundtrack" and the negative thought patterns and beliefs that are keeping your anxiety in place do so because they are *distorted*. In just the same way as a fun house mirror warps reality, your mind can warp what it perceives.

Cognitive distortions are inaccurate pictures of reality. Though it's possible to have a beneficial distortion, most of us have internal mental filters or biases that make us feel worse about ourselves, contribute to our anxiety, and increase the amount of misery we experience. Our mental processes are constantly working to sort through a great deal of data. Our brains are always looking for ways to get around obstacles and reduce the amount of mental work we have to do. Sometimes these shortcuts are useful, but sometimes they just jeopardize us.

How many different kinds of cognitive distortions are there? Well, in a way, there are as many distortions as there are possible thoughts! Below, we will have a look at some common "flavors," but we won't dwell on this since in the end this is not that important. What is important is recognizing that a distortion has occurred at all, and learning how to bring our perceptions back to reality.

As you read through the following list, see if some resonate with you—can you recognize them in any of your core beliefs or anxiety "soundtracks"? Chances are, you have a colorful blend of many all at once!

A Catalogue of Distortions

All-or-Nothing Thinking

All-or-nothing thinking, also called polarized thinking or black-and-white thinking, is the idea that everything can be seen in terms of two extremes that are opposites of each other. No middle ground, no shades of grey. This way of thinking is easy to spot because it uses absolute words like always, never, and forever.

Examples:

I'm a bad person.

He hates the whole thing.

It's completely impossible and always will be.

Overgeneralization

This is a broad statement incorrectly made about a specific situation. It takes a single instance and over-extrapolates to all situations, at all times, everywhere.

Examples:

I never do anything right (when you do one thing wrong).

The world is going down the tube (when you drop your toast on the floor).

People are cruel (when one person has been cruel to you).

Mental Filter

As we've already seen, a mental filter is simply a skewed way of thinking. It's like wearing a tinted pair of glasses or listening to a particular soundtrack play over your life. Or, it's like having unconscious expectations about what life is and can be.

Examples:

Oh, here's some mail that arrived. I wonder what they want now.

I've submitted it, but they probably won't even see my application.

She said nothing, so I know she's mad at me.

Disqualifying the Positive

When you have a fixed negative idea of the world, you unconsciously look for evidence that supports it. When you encounter evidence that suggests otherwise, you ignore it or find a way to make it support the view of the world you already have. You never take any credit for your own success, always saying that it was just a fluke or the result of things outside of you. Incidentally, this can overlap significantly with a lack of gratitude: "I know I have a brilliant job, three perfect children, an amazing house, good health, a loving family, and a million dollars in the bank... but *other than that*, everything is rotten."

More examples:

The first three successes were beginner's luck, and the fourth one was a fluke (plus, I just plain forgot about the fifth!).

He asked for a second date, so I bet he feels sorry for me.

It's just a measly award. Anyone could have won it.

Jumping to Conclusions and Fortune Telling

We take a few small bits of information and run with them, making inferences and assumptions that aren't really warranted. It's like filling in the blanks—but in a bad way.

Examples:

I didn't get the job, so I guess I better get ready to live in a box under a bridge for the rest of my life.

She didn't like her gift. I've completely blown it.

The doctor hasn't called yet, so maybe that means the test results are really bad.

Mind Reading

Assumption again, by a different name. In the absence of concrete information, we guess what people are thinking or feeling, or assume what their motivations are.

Examples:

I've been dumped again. They must all think I'm a boring person.

Everyone at that group dislikes me (despite having met everyone just once).

She said that just to rile me up (guessing at motivation).

Magnification or Minimization

This is just exaggerating or underestimating how likely something is to happen or how important it is. Since it's anxiety we're talking about, these distortions tend to happen in whatever direction makes the situation look worse.

Examples:

This is the worst thing that has ever happened to a human being ever.

My parents wouldn't even notice if I disappeared off the face of the earth.

My entire marriage meant nothing.

Emotional Reasoning

This is when we focus on the emotional content of an experience and assume that it accurately reflects the truth of a situation. This can be a tricky one to spot, but psychological distance helps us see that our interpretation of an event and the event are two different things. This goes hand in hand with personalization, where we assume that everything that happens directly relates to us somehow. For example, your son does badly at school and you immediately think that this says something about your parenting.

More examples:

I felt embarrassed; therefore, I must have been acting in an embarrassing manner.

I feel guilty about this, so I must actually be to blame.

I have a suspicion, and that's proof that something is really going on.

Now, as you read through all the above, you likely saw the overlap between them. **That's**

because all distortions have one thing in common: the deliberate misinterpretation of stimuli to serve a conclusion that is negative or threatening. If you've ever talked to someone with a really stubborn distortion, you may have even seen this deliberate attempt play out before your eyes—No matter what you say, it's like the other person *wants* to hold on to a certain perspective, and they will do whatever they can to land up there. That, in a nutshell, is what anxiety is.

The Triple Column Exercise

The triple column exercise can be done in just a few minutes per day once you've learned to recognize your own most common and most recurrent cognitive distortions. It's an approach that is much-loved by cognitive behavioral therapists because it helps you pinpoint all that negative programming that is in the background of your anxiety.

You can do the following in your head, but putting it on paper will silence that critical voice and produce much better results. What's more, having a written record can come in handy later when you want to see how far you've come and track your progress. The exercise can be done any time, or specifically when you're feeling that your thinking is getting a bit blurred. You could try it in the mornings to get set off on the right foot, or in the evenings to de-stress and offload.

1. **Take a sheet of paper and divide it into three columns, or create an Excel document or Google Spreadsheet and do the same.**
2. **The first column is for an "automatic thought" or entrenched belief.** By now you should be getting good at noticing when this self-sabotaging negative inner talk crops up. Don't worry if you don't feel like you always have a discrete single thought in sentence form. Just try to capture the essence, being as detailed or as general as you like.
3. **See if you can identify any distortions in the first column, and write them in the second column.** Don't underestimate how illuminating it can be just to put your thoughts down in black and white! You could have more than one

distortion, or even perhaps identify one that isn't on the list above—that's okay too.

4. **In the last column, you are going to carefully create a more "rational alternative."** This is your chance to slow down, be mindful, and think clearly. Take the thought and see what it could look like without the distortion applied to it. Think of another way to look at the situation that doesn't produce anxiety or other negative emotions.

That's the basic framework, now let's look at how we could use it with a real-life example:

In the first column, you could write *I had the worst day at work today. My pitch completely flopped, and my supervisor is going to be really mad I didn't make a good impression. I won't be surprised if I'm fired tomorrow.*

Your column may be filled with short phrases and words, or much longer descriptions. You might also find yourself listing out several different thoughts in bullet points. It's up to you.

Just get it all out, and when you think you've covered it, go into analysis mode and look for any distortions. In the second column, you could then possibly note down four different distortions going on: overgeneralization, all-or-nothing thinking, mental filter, and jumping to conclusions—there may be a bit of mind reading and fortune telling in there, too!

The final column is where things get interesting. Take your time with it, and don't rush ahead with what you think you "should" feel instead. **Walk yourself through each assumption and interpretation and ask for evidence, looking to see if there is another way to frame it all.** For example:

My pitch completely flopped—Could this be an exaggeration? "Flopped" is putting it strongly and not technically true, since there were one or two things that actually did go well. So it's more accurate to say *I could have done better* or *The presentation was fine, but not brilliant this time.*

My supervisor is going to be mad—Now, this may well be true. But do you 100 percent know this yet? Is it possible they may feel some other way, such as disappointed, confused, or mildly unimpressed—but not mad? Is it even possible that your supervisor found some parts of the pitch good? In cases like this, it can be very rational to simply say, *I'm not yet sure how my supervisor feels, but she hasn't actually said anything.*

I'm going to get fired tomorrow—another exaggeration and definitely jumping to conclusions. There's a bit of all-or-nothing thinking here, so ask yourself if there is some grey area before being fired outright. Maybe your boss is unhappy but simply says, "Please try harder next time," and that's the end of it? You change the thought to, *There's a chance my supervisor wants a word with me, but it's highly unlikely I'll be fired.*

As you read what you've put in the third column, maybe it dawns on you that you've done plenty of pitches in the past that have been really successful. In your anxious state of mind, you forgot about those. You also forget how much positive feedback you've received from your supervisor mere weeks before, not to mention the fact that you've actually had a few rotten pitches without it completely jeopardizing your job security.

Now, the next time you catch yourself feeling anxious about what's coming tomorrow, or find yourself ruminating over the pitch, you can bring out your three columns and remind yourself of the more rational alternative.

The triple column exercise may seem too easy on the surface. It can be tempting to think that because of its simplicity, it couldn't seriously change your mindset—but it can! This is because slowing down and actually putting thoughts down has a way of bringing your awareness to them in a way that doesn't happen with automatic thoughts and assumptions.

The more you try this exercise, the more you will find yourself challenging your anxious thoughts automatically. You may start to notice the same old distortions appearing again and again. Except every time you recognize it and call it out, it weakens somewhat and becomes even easier to recognize the next time around. Before you know it, you might catch yourself defaulting to the more rational alternative automatically.

Chapter 8: Reality Testing

Sigmund Freud was the first to coin the term "reality testing." **In essence, this is a way to make a clear distinction between your own thoughts, hopes, wishes, fears, and ideas about an event and reality itself**. This is actually a pretty rare ability! If we can see reality for what it is, then we gain an enormous advantage over ourselves when it comes to self-defeating patterns like rumination and anxiety.

We already employed a form of structured reality testing in the previous chapter, where we gradually asked ourselves whether our automatic thoughts really stood up to further scrutiny. This is the "testing" part, where **we actively look for**

alternative explanations, dial down our assumptions, and ask if we actually have any evidence for our conclusions. It turns our anxieties into something we have to handle and manage, rather than something enormous that we are trapped inside of.

Some people even give the voice of reality testing an identity. They imagine that they have an internal "cheerleader" or wise inner sage that is always looking out for them and always sees things clearly. This is the opposite of the inner critic and frequently argues against it. They get in the habit of not trusting their first mental impulse, but running it past this wiser, higher self first to see if it passes the test.

Here's what reality testing looks like:

You first think, *My friend saw me in the street but ignored me. He must really dislike me, after all. Maybe he was hoping I didn't see him and didn't want to talk to me.*

Upon reality testing, you think instead, *Maybe there's another explanation. Maybe he didn't see me at all. Or maybe he didn't greet me just because he's in a hurry and didn't have time to talk, but didn't want to be rude.*

Or you first think, *I messed up my first pottery lesson and didn't finish my bowl in time. The teacher thinks I'm the worst student she's had, and probably doesn't even want me to come back.*

On second thought, you moderate this and come up with an alternative: *Be rational—she is a beginner's pottery teacher. Her whole job is to work with people who don't yet know how to do pottery! There is no logical reason for her not to want me to return. Her business depends on it. Also, just because I don't know how to do pottery right now, it doesn't mean I can't learn. After all, that was the whole point of joining a class. I wouldn't need to go to a class if I could do it perfectly already.*

The big thing about reality testing is that it is not automatic. Call it human nature, but **most of us have the more negative, repetitive, and self-defeating thoughts on autopilot, whereas the more supportive ones take conscious effort**. Reality testing is simply giving yourself enough space to think of something different. It's about not taking your own word for it. Think of it as a kind of meta-thinking—you don't just trust the first knee-jerk thing that pops into your head, but rather you have high standards for your thoughts. They need to actually be true before you entertain them!

Luckily for us, this is a skill we can learn and strengthen. It's perfectly okay to have an automatic negative thought at first—but it doesn't mean that you can't follow it with something better, something you choose mindfully. So how do we do it?

Three Ways to Put Your Thoughts to the Test

Be Objective

You're seeing one perspective. What about the other perspectives? Try to see a situation from as many points of view as possible. What could the other person be thinking? What would an objective, neutral bystander say?

Take your time. Often, we make snap decisions and judgments about how we feel or what a situation means. But there is no rush and no reason you can't slow down and think through things systematically. Be like a scientist or a lawyer in your style of thought—don't accept anything unless there's a good reason to.

Always remember that other people live in their own worlds just as you live in yours. They have their own feelings, thoughts, priorities, filters, biases, and ways of assigning meaning. Before you mind read or make assumptions about someone, try to appreciate that other people's minds are often not really accessible to you.

Think First and then React

It is not a foregone conclusion that you *must* react to any situation or stimulus. It is not inevitable that you have an emotion about what is unfolding, or that you are forced to act on that emotion. The truth is, there is a big space between a stimulus and your response to it. In that space lies your choice—and you can choose to do nothing at all.

On the other hand, you might decide that you are not doing enough, i.e., you are stressing and worrying and ruminating, but not actually *doing* anything to help your situation. Perhaps you have confused feeling and emotion with taking action. How many of us unconsciously think that as long as we were worried about something, that this somehow counts as doing something to fix the problem? But you can choose how much emotion you want to express or indulge. Why not ask how much emotion a situation *requires* and go from there, rather than assuming that if you feel it, there's nothing to do but keep on feeling it?

Then, when you act, your action is from an informed, conscious place. You are active and not reactive.

Seek External Points of View

You are not in a strange void floating in space, having to grasp at straws of meaning. There are "anchors" all around you onto which you can attach your perception and ground yourself. One obvious way to do this? Ask others.

It's worth checking your perception against others not because they are likely to be more "right" than you, but because becoming aware of other perspectives reminds you that *you* have a perspective too, and it may be just as wrong as other people's sometimes seem to us! It's only when you slow down and become aware of your thoughts that you can see just how many assumptions you make. But you always have the option of comparing these assumptions against other peoples'.

"I saw you on the street yesterday and you didn't greet me. I guessed that you were upset, but I thought it was better to ask you."

"Upset? Oh no—I don't even remember seeing you at all. I must have been completely distracted with something else!"

Perhaps you're now wondering if reality testing always disproves the mental theory you currently have running. There seems to be an unspoken rule in CBT circles that reality is always less scary than you think it is, and your perceptions are always inaccurate. But let's be real here: Unless you are completely detached from reality, there will always be *some* truth to *some* of your perceptions. What then?

First, understand that reality testing is not a way of "talking yourself down." It's not a way to self-soothe or convince you that everything is going to be okay (even and especially if it isn't going to be okay!). You are not practicing telling yourself a nice lie, but really looking at reality as it is. That means that occasionally, you will test an idea and find that it is pretty close to "real." Very occasionally you will discover that you *under*estimated a certain idea or concept.

But this is not a problem. **Being a non-anxious person is not about living a life free of threat or difficulty. Rather, it's about refining your relationship to reality so that you are clear-sighted, accepting, and realistic**. If you discover that a situation really is quite dire, then so be it—reality testing will help you find the appropriate level of panic. Why worry more than you need to, right?

In fact, the answer to the question "how much anxiety is the right amount?" is "zero." There will be times in life when you need to be cautious or alert or humble or shrewd. There will be times when you need to draw on inner reserves of resilience to get through a challenge. There will be feelings of sadness or anger. However, pure anxiety is not ever necessary or useful in any amount. So, for an example, imagine that you are worried to death that you may have cancer. It is no use to be anxious about it since worrying doesn't change the outcome. But let's say you actually *do* have cancer. Guess what? Worrying about it still doesn't change a thing.

Distinguishing between Your Thoughts and Someone Else's

Without reality testing, you risk getting carried away on a sea of overwhelming thoughts. If you have no way to test the veracity of a thought that pops up into your world, it can invade your mind and take over. Negative thoughts can be powerful, and before you know it, you are buying into them, forgetting that you are not looking at realty but a thought *about* reality.

One sneaky way this can happen is via other people's thoughts. Have you ever gotten really stressed out because of another person's actions? Have you ever felt anxious because someone else was anxious, and you couldn't help but get caught up in that dynamic with them? Consider the example of a husband who knows his wife is meant to leave in five minutes to go to her doctor's appointment, but she hasn't even showered and dressed yet. He watches and grows anxious, worried that she'll be late. When the wife does leave late in a panic, he is completely overwhelmed and stressed out. He thinks things like "I live in a mad house" and "this always happens."

While it's true that the wife is late, it's actually not his problem at all. And yet he internalizes that stress and makes it a part of his world, with his cognitive distortions overgeneralizing to cover his own life in the stressful filter that more correctly belongs to his wife. Consider the same couple who are at a restaurant later that day. The husband is in a bad mood and behaving rudely to the waiter. The wife feels guilty and embarrassed on his behalf and begins to feel anxious. When the waiter gets her order wrong, she thinks, *He did it on purpose because he thinks we're rude customers.*

Can you see how both the husband and wife are allowing the other one's stress to seep into their own perceptions?

A little appreciated skill in anxiety-management is learning to recognize **what is yours and what is other people's.**

Of course, human beings are social creatures, and we are all interdependent and influence one another in good and bad ways. But if you struggle with anxiety, it's a good idea to routinely ask *you* if you are suffering from anxiety at all—or if you're more accurately suffering someone else's anxiety!

Have you incorrectly assumed responsibility for something that has nothing to do with you?

Are you allowing someone else's choices, actions, and decisions to control your life?

Have you substituted someone else's perspective, filter, or worldview for your own?

Are you letting someone else decide for you what things mean or what to focus on?

Are you mistakenly taking on other people's emotions as your own?

These are not easy questions to answer, but they will do the difficult work of separating reality from a whole world of hopes, assumptions, fears, and obligations. One great way to become better at managing your anxiety is to surround yourself with people who are themselves good at it. If you are routinely spending time with people who blur boundaries, encourage your cognitive distortions, or implicate you in their psychological dynamics, it's so much harder to remain clear and grounded.

This is why someone may make enormous strides in therapy and do good work to overcome their anxiety, but seem to hit square one the moment they go home over the holidays. It's because their home life may be a **complex web of anxious patterns**—the moment you step into that web, it is very difficult to do anything other than play the corresponding role. In other words, reality testing is infinitely more difficult if you are in a situation where other people are not connected to reality either! In these cases, a therapist can be a valuable ally and will help you unpick what is real and what is not.

Imagine a woman who has grown up in a family where all her relatives experience anxiety. Her mother may have been obsessed with staying safe, while her father had a kind of mental filter that saw the world as a hostile place. In a way, this woman's family has its own *shared set of cognitive distortions*. As she grows up and makes a life for herself, however, she has to look at this dynamic as objectively as possible.

She needs to see her parents' views as exactly that—views, and not an accurate picture of how the world is. Then she needs to decide what is *their* view and what is *hers*—i.e., untangle from old habits and thought patterns that she learned as a child. She can gradually come to realize that her mother's fear, for example, is not hers. When she spots this habitual fear response in herself, she gains the opportunity to make a different choice. She shares her experience with others, and realizes that her family's version of reality isn't quite "normal"—or at least it's not something she wants for herself.

In this way, reality testing can be the foundation of a deep, thorough rewriting of your entire life script. If this woman had merely learned a few relaxation techniques or said affirmations in the bathroom mirror, she would have coped with her anxiety. But she never would have learned where the anxiety came from in the first place. She would have never measured it up against reality.

Summary:

- Your brain can work against you if it runs on cognitive distortions, which are simply inaccurate pictures of reality. These can include overgeneralization, black-and-white thinking, emotional reasoning, discounting the positive, catastrophizing, or mind reading. Whatever they are or how they work, distortions are a deliberate misinterpretation of stimuli to serve a

conclusion that is negative or threatening. This leads to anxiety.
- The triple column exercise can help you identify and rewrite cognitive distortions, or replace them with something more rational. Note down the 1. Automatic thought, 2. The distortion, and 3. A rational alternative. Walk yourself through each assumption and interpretation and ask for evidence, looking to see if there is another way to frame events.
- Reality testing means making a clear distinction between your own thoughts, hopes, wishes, fears, and ideas about an event and reality itself. Actively look for alternative explanations, dial down assumptions, and look for evidence that counters a negative automatic reaction to stimuli.
- Look for a neutral, objective perspective; remember that there is a space between a stimulus and your response to it, and that you never *have to* react, so take your time to process; and finally, anchor yourself

in alternative and external points of view rather than assuming yours is gospel.
- Being non-anxious is not about living a life free of difficulty. It's a relationship to reality that is clear-sighted, accepting, and realistic.
- Lastly, recognize what anxiety is yours and what belongs to other people. Never substitute someone else's perspective as your own or take responsibility for their emotions or actions.

Part Four: Taking a Step Back

Chapter 9: The Batman Effect

When you live with anxiety and pay a lot of attention to that negative inner voice, it's as though you become a temporarily worse version of yourself. You become smaller, more fearful, doubtful, and pessimistic. A less confident, less creative, and less resilient version of yourself. **The "Batman effect" is basically the reverse of this—it's an attempt to not only counter your brain's own bias against you, but replace it with something that will actually work *for* you.**

The term comes from the fictional character Bruce Wayne's constant struggle to overcome problems as a normal person. He has his normal version of himself, but then he is also Batman, who is capable of so, so much more.

Studies have shown that when children pretend to be a competent and powerful character they know from film or TV, they persevere with boring tasks far longer, and they actually perform better than if they had simply tackled the tasks as themselves. This is a pretty big deal!

By putting themselves in the shoes of someone who is not fearful, unconfident, or incapable, it's as though the children learn to literally see the world from that perspective. Problems are easier to solve, and obstacles easier to deal with. **The Batman effect shows us the power of gaining "psychological distance" from our own limited ideas of who we are and what we are capable of.**

A 2016 study at the University of Minnesota showed how self-distance, or looking at your own situation from the point of view of an outsider, can increase persistence and resilience. In the study, children of four and six years old were given a task and asked to repeat it over and over for ten minutes. If they couldn't go on, they were offered a break and a game. When the kids took on the perspective of a superhero like Batman, they took fewer breaks and pressed on even when the task got challenging or repetitive. They took more breaks when they took a first-person point of view, i.e., acted as themselves.

Now, this may seem like a bit of a gimmick—can you *really* reduce your anxiety levels just by pretending you're a character who isn't anxious? It turns out the strategy of adopting an alter ego is actually a perfect way to gain some distance from strong emotions and look at a situation more objectively.

Rachel White, an assistant professor of psychology at Hamilton College in New York State, says that putting distance between ourselves and a challenging situation helps us think more clearly about it. It could be as simple as asking yourself "what would Batman do?"

She says it's a great idea to **choose a different alter ego for different goals or challenges**. She claims, "When I was a postdoc, we had a little saying in our lab that if you're an undergrad, pretend to be a grad student. If you are a grad student, pretend to be a postdoc, and if you're a postdoc, pretend to be the leader of the lab—just to get you to that next level."

This may be far more effective than robotically writing down affirmations or saying ready-made affirmations. Instead, why not have a morning ritual where you try on your alter ego's perspective? Have a piece of jewelry or lucky pair of socks that you pick for days you know will be challenging. Make the connection internally that when you wear these things, it's the same as a superhero putting on their cape.

How to Create a Non-anxious Alter Ego

The idea is to identify (or create from scratch) a persona that possesses the characteristics and traits that you are trying to develop in yourself. If you are anxious, this is likely someone who is:

Calm

Self-possessed

In control

Confident

Hopeful

Self-assured

Relaxed

Positive

Trusting

If you have a few favorite cognitive distortions, you could begin with those and ask what kind of a person does the opposite. If you have a habit of all-or-nothing thinking, for example, who can you think of (in real life or fiction) that is a master of nuanced, subtle thought? You can pick someone you literally know, or a famous role model from history. Alternatively, you could construct an alter ego from scratch. Beyonce explains how she created an alter ego to help her perform on stage—her name is Sasha Fierce and she allows the singer to tap into overflowing energy, confidence, and power.

"Usually when I hear the chords, when I put on my stilettos, like the moment right before when you're nervous . . . then Sasha Fierce appears, and my posture and the way I speak and everything is different," she told Oprah in an interview in 2008.

Spend some time really fleshing out your alter ego. They should be more than just an image in your mind, but a full person, with their own personality, thought processes, and ways of doing things. You might like to blend a few fictional characters or famous people together, or lean heavily on more primal archetypes like a warrior, a queen, or a sagely magician. You could even borrow from myth and religion and decide that your uber-calm alter ego is a blend of a serene bodhisattva, Mother Theresa, and a dragon that lives at the top of a mystical mountain.

Take your time conjuring the image of this alter ego in your imagination. What are they wearing? What is their facial expression, and how do they walk? What is their tone of voice, and what are they saying? What actions are they taking, and how do others respond?

Going deeper, what does this alter ego care about? If they had a motto or a catch phrase, what would it be? Think of a suitable name for them, and perhaps even associate them with a few symbols or related images. You might like to get creative with the name—for example, "Queen Sheba the Great" or "Master X, Overcomer of all Obstacles."

The reason you're going to all this effort is because, when it comes to the heat of the moment, you need to be able to know exactly how your character would act. This is not pure fantasy—you are trying to **find a way**

to bring this alter ego to life with real-world action. What would they do? What would they say? What aspects of the situation would they focus on? Commit to doing, saying, and focusing on the same things.

When you are mired in a stressful situation, all your old thought patterns may kick off automatically, and you may get quickly overwhelmed in negative emotions. But that's *you*—what about your alter ego? Call on them for help. It's easy for you to imagine that they are outside your situation and not overwhelmed by whatever is overwhelming you.

If this feels tricky, **ask instead what they might tell you if they were giving you advice**. Imagine a conversation with them, and picture them saying all the right things necessary to get you out of your predicament. What do they say? In this way, you leverage yourself out of a tricky situation and give yourself the chance to look at things through someone else's eyes. When we are trapped in anxiety, it can feel like an impossibility to see out of it. But then, with this technique, you don't have to see out of it at all. You just have to imagine someone who could. Clever, isn't it?

Another related study (Dolcos & Albarracin, 2014) asked participants to give themselves encouraging advice in second-person voice—for example, "You will focus on every question." This improved their performance on a task when compared to those who used first person ("I will do my best"). This goes to show that it's not the alter ego per se, but the psychological distance that is helping. So, instead of saying to yourself, "What am I going to do?" you could say, "You will find a way out of this, don't worry." This simple change in language alone is enough to give you a little space.

A final study led by professor of psychology Ethan Kross at the University of Michigan (Kross & Ayduk, 2016) shows that even small perspective shifts can have a big impact. The experiment had participants thinking about an upcoming challenge in their future—for example, an exam. One group was asked to think about the event by immersing themselves completely in it, while the other group was asked to think about it in a distanced way, i.e., imagining that they were on the outside and looking in.

The differences were impressive. Those who saw the whole thing as though they were a fly on the wall felt far less anxiety and also rated themselves as more competent at dealing with the perceived challenge. They ended up adopting healthier coping mechanisms and finding more pro-active solutions.

To try this for yourself, simply change your inner talk from first to third person—for example, "Jon is feeling unsure about . . ." instead of "I feel unsure . . ." Rather than saying "I feel terrified," you might say "there is a feeling of fear at the moment" and remove yourself from the equation entirely. By adding "right now" or "at the moment," you are similarly putting time limits on a situation, showing that the situation is not permanent and all-encompassing.

Learn what your alter ego has to teach you.

Your alter ego is not just a great way to get around anxiety. It can be used any time you feel like your ordinary ways of looking at things are limiting you. Why not combine your alter ego with that little voice inside that challenges assumptions and asks for evidence?

Your ego may say: "You can't do that. What will people think?"

But your alter ego says: "Who says that what they think matters? What do *you* think?"

Your ego may jump in with: "Don't do it. You'll fail and make a fool of yourself."

Your alter ego won't let you get away with it, and says: "Who says you'll fail? I'm curious; it looks fun. Let's do it!"

Your ego may say: "This is really bad..."

But your alter ego says: "Nah! It's nothing I can't handle."

Interestingly, Beyonce now claims she no longer needs Sasha Fierce, and that she stopped calling on her help around 2010 (incidentally, a year later, the singer Adele claimed she created her own alter ego called Sasha Carter—a blend of Sasha Fierce and singer June Carter). What we can conclude from this is that over time, Beyonce really became Sasha Fierce. The alter ego was a psychological crutch, but once she learned those skills, the alter ego was no longer necessary.

The same thing may happen with you. By repeatedly asking yourself what your non-anxious alter ego would do, it starts to become automatic. Eventually, what they would do and what you would do are the same.

Chapter 10: Learning to Tolerate Uncertainty

Uncertainty is a part of life. We are never, ever in the position to be certain about what will happen tomorrow or a month from now. We can never truly know what others are thinking or how life would have looked if we had made a different decision. And when times are tough, none of us mere mortals can predict how things will pan out, or what the best, risk-free way forward is.

However, people do seem to vary significantly in their ability to tolerate this fact of life. "Uncertainty tolerance" is a variable in a person's psychological makeup, just like a peanut allergy or an inability to digest lactose. If you have issues with anxiety, chances are you are one of those people who have a very low threshold for uncertainty.

Is that a problem? Not really. Most of us like a little familiarity, routine, and predictability in life. It's why we order the same things at restaurants, wake up at the same time each day, and prefer talking to people we already know instead of strangers. There's nothing wrong with being uncomfortable with the unknown or the novel—that is, until there is something wrong with it. Anxiety is a sign that your intolerance for uncertainty has gone a little too far.

If you're allergic to a food, your body goes into an extreme reactive mode—you wheeze, your throat closes, maybe you break out in hives or start coughing or even go into shock. It's the same for uncertainty tolerance. Your mind goes into an extreme reactive mode, and you do whatever you can to avoid and manage that feeling of uncertainty. Only, this reaction is more of a problem than the uncertainty will ever be.

There are loads of things people do when they're trying to make the unknown known or the uncertain certain:

- You may obsessively seek reassurance from other people, either checking their opinions or asking them to tell you that everything is or will be okay. Comparing perspectives or asking for help is one thing, but reassurance-seeking becomes a problem when you keep doing it . . . and it doesn't seem to soothe you, anyway.
- You prefer to do tasks yourself just so you can be sure that they are done properly, and you won't have to leave it to someone else. This feels like a good way to manage stress, but often makes more of it, since you end up doing everything.
- You may do "research" in an effort to gather as much information as possible so that the unknown feels a little less scary. You Google a problem to death or sit with a journal and make a dozen pros and cons lists, or try to force an ambiguous situation by breaking it down on a page.
- You might be a very busy, active person who can never sit still. You

might like the feeling of always having something to do, as at least this means that you're being proactive and are not at the mercy of random, unknown events that you can't control. Distraction can be a classic way to avoid having to sit with the sheer uncertainty of a situation.

- Avoidance can make you turn down novel experiences, avoid potentially good opportunities, and live a life that lacks spontaneity. Think of the person who would rather spoil a nice surprise by knowing what it is immediately, than tolerate a moment of anticipation and mystery.
- You may constantly check and confirm to make sure plans are going ahead, or to check up on people. You may go over emails and messages a million times to check for mistakes (a little like some people need to check that the door is locked twenty times before they can leave the house).

Naturally, there *are* some genuine ways to reduce uncertainty in life. If you are anxious because you have an important event tomorrow and you don't know whether it will rain, you could always read the forecast and prepare yourself. But what about if you waste an hour reading every forecast you can find? What if you waste another hour talking to people about how worried you are about rain and asking for them to reassure you that it will probably be fine? What if you get so sick with worry that you decide to cancel the event entirely because you can't handle not knowing?

The truth is, the behaviors we engage in to try to reduce uncertainty are the real problem—not the uncertainty itself. Why? Because for the most part, **it is impossible to get rid of uncertainty**. What we can do, however, is get better at tolerating it (or even relishing it and using it for our own benefit).

Acting "As If"
One way to become more tolerant of uncertainty is to act "as if" you already are. The idea here is that you first change the outward behavior, and in time, you will eventually change the way you think and feel about uncertainty. The reason for approaching things this way around is

because it's quite difficult to convince yourself to just change your attitude. You've probably had people tell you things like: "Relax, there's nothing you can do, so why worry, right?" While you may have agreed on a cognitive level, it doesn't seem to do much to get rid of the anxiety you feel!

In CBT, our thoughts, feelings, and actions are connected. That means that we can change any one of them, and it will affect the others. Here's a way that acting "as if" can help you raise your tolerance threshold for the unknown.

Step 1: Identify the behaviors

As always, begin by shining the light of awareness on all the ways anxiety is currently showing up in your life. Focus on those behaviors that are an attempt to reduce the discomfort of uncertainty.
This will take some honesty.

Do you tend to seek reassurance? Or are you a double checker? Perhaps when faced with uncertainty, your reaction is to delay, avoid, or procrastinate. Maybe you get bogged down in reassurance and need to check everyone else's opinion before you decide what to do.

It can be tricky to uncover these behaviors because they are likely automatic and ingrained. But you will be alerted to their presence every time you feel anxious and like you're "in the dark" about something. That looming uncertainty, the scary unknown, or the feeling of something ambiguous or vague in the future that has not been resolved yet—this is the kind of emotion that triggers avoidance behavior. So to catch the behavior, look closely for moments you feel the sting of uncertainty, and watch closely to see what your response is.

An example: You're thinking about leaving your job and re-training in a completely new area. Surprise! The outcome of doing so is uncertain. You notice yourself feeling primarily fear—you're worried you're making a mistake, you keep asking "what if" questions and catastrophizing (hello, cognitive distortions!), and you keep thinking that the whole process would be so much easier if you knew without doubt that the risk of leaving would be worth it, and you'd be guaranteed a good outcome. You notice these feelings of anxiety. Then you notice what you're doing to avoid them whenever they come up—you go into "research mode."

Are you familiar with research mode? It's something that *looks* useful and intelligent on the surface, but it's really just a way to prolong anxiety! You notice that you essentially try to guess what your future will look like so that it's no longer unknown. You spend hours online looking at the stats for your new line of work, you fill journals with lists, you pick apart and analyze every possibility, etc.

Step 2: Rank the behaviors

Look at the behaviors you've identified. Now imagine that you could *not* do these behaviors—how anxious would you feel? So, in our example, imagine that you could no longer go online and Google things like "percentage of cyber security experts that are unemployed." Let's say not being able to do so would make you feel anxiety on a level of about five or six. Not being able to make another pros and cons list would create anxiety of about a level three, and so on. Do this for all the anxiety-avoiding behaviors you've identified. Then, put them in order from least to most anxious.

When you are living "as if" you are tolerant of anxiety, it's a good idea to start small and work your way up. Otherwise, you might get overwhelmed and cause the opposite effect—i.e., create so much anxiety you cling to avoidance behaviors even more.

Step 3: Start practicing being more tolerant

Beginning at the low end of the list (the things that are least anxious), pick a few behaviors and challenge yourself to forego doing them, and experience the anxiety, anyway. At first, start with around three tasks or behaviors a week, then stop to evaluate. The goal here is not to torture yourself. It's not really about what you're NOT doing, but about what you are—i.e., tolerating uncertainty. So as you deliberately avoid the behavior, focus on facing the anxious feelings head on and seeing what it feels like not to rush in to try to escape or avoid them.

In our example, you might catch yourself thinking about your new career one afternoon and feel so much anxiety that you are immediately tempted to ask your friend if they think you're being crazy and what they would do (reassurance seeking). But you notice the anxiety, you notice the impulse to escape it, and you deliberately choose not to. Remember the Batman effect? Try telling yourself to behave as a person with high uncertainty tolerance would behave. If it feels like you're just pretending, that's fine!

Step 4: Track your progress

How did it feel to just "sit with" anxiety? Did you notice the feelings increasing or decreasing? If they eventually faded, how long did it take? What helped? As you keep repeating the process, do you find that tolerating uncertainty is getting easier?

Periodically challenge yourself to move up the anxiety list and forego more behaviors and tolerate higher levels of anxiety. Remember that you are always in control. Nobody is forcing you to do it, and you can stop at any time—but try to stay at least a little curious about what it feels like to behave like someone who isn't afraid of the unknown. Sure, you don't have to like the experience. But is it always as bad as you think?

The big illusion with avoidance behaviors is that they are keeping you safe or helping you solve problems. But when you stop yourself from indulging in them, you may see that things largely remain the same whether you fret about them or not. You may naturally decide in that case not to bother fretting!

Naturally, things will sometimes not turn out well. You may discover you try one of the tasks on your list and regret not doing the avoidance behavior. That's okay. Slow down and look carefully at what happened, why, and how you felt. If you allow some uncertainty in your life, things *will* occasionally go wrong. But stay curious— how did you react when they went wrong? How bad was the outcome? Was it completely unfixable, or were you able to adapt and adjust? Notice how you are perfectly capable of coping *even if you're not 100 percent prepared or in control.* This is a realization you won't allow yourself to have if you always insist on taking control.

Sometimes, there is an assumption at the core of uncertainty intolerance that goes

like this: "I cannot cope if things go wrong; therefore, I have to do my best to stop them from going wrong." But the "as if" exercise gives you a chance to prove to yourself that you actually can be resilient, creative, and adaptive. Even if things don't go according to plan, you can respond in healthy ways. What's more, you may realize that even if things do turn out poorly, they do so accidentally—in other words, it was something you could not have avoided even if you had engaged in all your habitual ways.

Remember to go slow and be kind to yourself. Anxiety and preference for the familiar are not a bad thing and, in a certain dose, are perfectly normal. As you find out what that normal level is, go gently and practice self-compassion. It took a lifetime for you to develop those uncertainty-avoidance behaviors—they won't change overnight!

Chapter 11: Externalization

Understanding the timeline your anxiety plays out across, using the ABCDE method, stepping outside of your brain to look carefully at its cognitive distortions, reality testing, and the Batman technique—all of these approaches have one major thing in common. **They all work because they act to separate us from our anxious experience and put distance between us and that feeling.** And that's why they all work.

In this chapter, we'll be looking more closely at the idea of **externalization**, which is any time we are able to connect to the world *outside* of our currently anxious experience. Externalization is like a little peephole through which we can see a glimpse of something different—the possibility of a non-anxious way of being.

Sometimes, just being cognizant of the fact that you are anxious and that you don't necessarily have to be is all it takes to knock you of that fixation. That's because anxiety is a narrowing of perception. If you can open your perception again, you reduce the anxiety.

Throughout the chapters of this book, we have considered many different ways to contextualize the anxiety response, to take a step back and get a different view on it, or to put different filters over it. This is not just so we can be free of unpleasant negative emotions, but also so that we can better experience positive ones. Without anxiety (or should we say, with healthy levels of anxiety), you are free to be more of who you are, to take good risks, to explore and create, to change and evolve, and to enjoy living your life as a valuable person with unique talents and useful insights.

So many people talk about eliminating or reducing anxiety (including in this book!), but sometimes, all that's needed is to just change the way we are looking at it. Externalization sounds simple, but once you really understand what it's about, you may be astonished by just how powerful a force it really is. Here are a few more ways to use externalization to disentangle from your anxiety once and for all.

When a problem is internalized, it's difficult to see it clearly. This is like being on street-level in some strange, new city and feeling completely lost. You look down alleyways, but you don't know how far along they go or where they lead to. You're not quite sure how bad your predicament is since you can't tell the way out or if you're making any progress. If you've ever been badly lost, you'll recognize one particular sensation that also occurs with anxiety: the sinking feeling that a bad situation could go on forever and ever.

Externalizing, however, is getting a different view on the problem. In this example, it's like zooming high up into the air and looking down on yourself inside that city. You are still in the city, but you can now see the city's edges and can clearly find a way out. The problem suddenly has a definite size and shape, and there is the promise of a solution.

Compare this example with the following statements:

1. I am an anxious person.
2. I am experiencing anxiety right now.

The speaker of the first sentence is completely identified with their situation, internalized and enmeshed with the anxiety. They are trapped in a city and cannot even begin to think that there are other places in the world they could be. The speaker of the second sentence is outside their experience. They are still anxious, but the anxiety is not the total of their experience and is not a defining feature of their entire personality.

In the first, you *are* your experience. In the second, you are *having* an experience (which means there is the possibility to NOT have it). In the first, anxiety is everything. In the second, it is just one thing that is happening. Small change in perspective, but big difference!

How Narrative Therapy Can Help

One way to get outside of the story of anxiety is to start becoming the *teller* of that story, rather than an *actor* simply playing their part. Enter narrative therapy. Narrative therapy is usually best attempted with a qualified professional, but we can certainly take inspiration from their methods. With this kind of therapy, your psychologist helps you **separate yourself from your problem, and then reconnect to your skills and abilities** so that you're better able to navigate that problem—on your own terms. Here are a few easy ways to start doing this for yourself.

Tip 1: Think of anxiety as an outside force rather than a personality trait

Anxiety is something you experience, not something you are. Try to get out of the mindset of labeling and diagnosing yourself, especially by saying things like "I'm anxious" or "I'm a worrier." Instead, think of anxiety more as a temporary event—like weather. Go into descriptive mode rather than labeling mode. For example, instead of saying "I'm a worrier," describe what is actually happening in the moment: "My heart is beating. I can see my mind returning to the same idea over and over again." This is value neutral and objective.

Tip 2: Give your anxiety a label, not yourself

As we've already seen, it can be helpful to give yourself an alter ego that possesses all the abilities you are trying to develop in yourself. But you can also name and shame your anxiety itself. There's a well-established literary tradition of calling depression a "black dog." Why not give your anxiety a name and personality too? All the better if you can diminish how serious and scary it is by giving it a ridiculous name or appearance—think of a small, nerdy gremlin-like creature named Neville who you get into the habit of telling, "Thanks for trying to help, Neville, but be quiet, I'm busy." This way, anxiety is like a bad house guest who comes to visit occasionally, rather than a permanent part of who you are.

Tip 3: Acknowledge what anxiety is costing you

When you are fully identified with and engrossed in your anxiety, it seems like the most natural and obvious thing in the world—like you couldn't imagine not doing it. What's harder to remember is that anxiety also has negative effects on you. It's worth reminding yourself in the moment of the impact that anxiety is really having on you, your work, your relationships, your self-esteem, etc. This does two things. First, it stops you from getting too drawn into your anxiety and brings you back to reality. Second, it helps you predict when it will show up so you can adjust accordingly.

For example, "Anxiety is making me less efficient at work. I know it will try to show up at my presentation today, so I'm going to make sure I'm ready for it when it does. I may get anxious, but I'm also still an effective person who is good at my job, and that's important to me." A big part of narrative therapy is remembering the resources you have: all the skills, experience, values, talents, and relationships you have to help and support you.

Tip 4: Remind yourself of your values

Anxiety is awful because it can diminish who we are. On one hand, we might value our relationships, our career, and learning new things, and on the other hand, there is anxiety forcing us to behave in ways that don't fit our principles or what we know our goals are. Another way to externalize anxiety is not just to detach it from you, but more strongly attach to all those things that *are* working for you right now.

Anxiety is difficult and challenging. But what else makes you who you are? What is your unique contribution to the world, or the thing you care most about? What fires you up and makes life meaningful and interesting to you? These are the things to identify with!

Imagine that someone is terrified of networking, meeting new people, and promoting themselves. This could mean they hide in the shadows and never take any risks to advance their business. But if they can remember why they started their business in the first place, the meaning they placed in that achievement, and how it speaks to their deepest goals, they can push through the anxiety.

You Don't Have to be Free of Anxiety

It is human to feel anxiety sometimes. It is normal to experience challenge and difficulty and to constantly grapple with fears and personal weaknesses. It's worth restating this: There is no problem with being an imperfect being or with experiencing unhappiness.

When you externalize your anxiety (or any other problem, for that matter), you are not saying that it magically disappears or that you are no longer bothered by it. It may still prove challenging, and you may not like it any more than you did when you were completely overwhelmed by it. The secret is: it doesn't matter. You don't have to completely get rid of anxiety. You only have to learn to manage it. People who have overcome their anxiety problems have not turned into steel men who are invulnerable, fearless, and able to achieve anything. In fact, they may be even more willing than the anxious person to fully experience their negative emotions. What makes the difference is that they have understood their anxiety, befriended it, and kept it at arm's length where it can be managed and moderated.

You could begin to treat your occasional anxiety like you treat a mole on your face or a scratch on your car. It's not great, but you accept it, and it's not the end of the world. It doesn't define you, and it doesn't limit you. Of course you do what you can to make sure it doesn't bother you more than it should, but once you've done that, you forget about it and carry on with other things in life that truly deserve your attention. If you ask anyone who has made drastic changes in their life where anxiety is concerned, they will tell you that it is always there, in a way. But *they* have changed. Their attitude, their focus, and their coping mechanisms are different, and so the anxiety just doesn't matter quite as much as it used to.

What Does Your Anxiety Mean?

Narrative therapy has broader uses, too. Compare the following two accounts:

1. "My anxiety just started up for no reason in my twenties, and I hated it. It cost me so many opportunities. I was always on the back foot, always nervous, trying my best to hide it from others. I always felt it was unfair that

it should have happened to me. Maybe I have stress genes that come from my mother's side of the family, I don't know. I just pray that one day it will finally fade a little, but who knows..."

2. "I think my anxiety developed as a response to all the pressures that kicked in after I left the university. Looking back, I know it was my way of coping, but I'm learning new ways of coping now. It was hard, but I think it taught me to regulate my emotions in a way I wouldn't have otherwise. It taught me to be grateful. At the end of the day, it has reminded me not to take anything for granted. It's surprising, but anxiety has made me so much stronger."

In the first account, the person is not only fully identified with their anxiety, they are *passive*. They don't know where it comes from, why it happens, or what it means. They are simply at its mercy. Experiencing anxiety is seen as a fatalistic thing ("stress genes") and the whole thing is felt to be unintelligible and random . . . hence, there's not a lot you can do about it but pray.

In the second account, anxiety is not seen this way at all. The person is instead *making meaning of their experiences*. They put the anxiety in context and "own" it, finding out what can be learned from the experience and how to move on proactively and consciously. They are not passively waiting for someone to tell them what is wrong with them or what their experiences mean—they are choosing to do this for themselves, and in a positive way.

This is one of the powers of narrative therapy. Consider a challenging event: a car accident. In Story One, the car accident is one of many bad luck events that occur without reason to a poor victim. It is something that merely happens to them. In Story Two, the car accident is pivotal, but the events that come before and after put the whole thing in context. The suffering, the stress, the shock—*all of it is redeemed because it means something.* In Story Two, the negative emotions are easier to bear because they are a part of a bigger story that has a happy, life-affirming ending. In Story One, there is no such redeeming context.

So here is the question—**can you look at the challenges and negative events in**

your life and create a narrative around them according to your own values?

If you can do so, then you are no longer a passive victim waiting to see what life inflicts on you. Instead, you are an active participant of life and a co-creator of its meaning. You don't ask "why me?!" but instead ask "I wonder what I can learn from this?"

If you can do so, you might also find that it's easier to be compassionate with yourself when looking back at your life. We all construct stories about who we are and what our lives have meant. If we have let anxiety get the better of us, sometimes we can create stories about ourselves that are very disempowering. But it is always possible to take a nobler, kinder attitude to the overall story arc of your life. Think about the attitude shift required to say things like:

"I did the best I could with what I had at the time."
"I'm still learning."
"Negative events give meaning and purpose to my life. They make me stronger. They teach me. They challenge me."

"Ultimately I'm not afraid of what life may bring in the future."

Compare this with:

"I did what I did because I had no choice. None of this is up to me."
"I can't do it and I'll never figure it out."
"I hate the negative things that have happened to me. I can't cope. I am under threat, and every challenge may be the one that destroys me."
"I live in fear. I'm not in charge."

This is perhaps the deepest perspective shift we can make, and it may take a lifetime. The way we do it is to connect with the things we hold most dear to our souls and allow that to infuse meaning and worth into the lives we are living. Trauma counselors have long known that "meaning-making" is an invaluable part of processing pain from the past. When we are able to look at all the dark parts of our lives and reclaim them, we put ourselves back in charge. When we can reframe our worst traits, our anxiety, our fearfulness, and our low self-worth as a necessary stepping stone on the way to something better, we take charge of our own narratives. It is the biggest and best way we can externalize from our suffering.

Summary:

- The Batman effect helps us get "psychological distance" from our own limited ideas of who we are and what we are capable of. Working with an alter ego can help us push back against ingrained negative biases we have toward ourselves.
- Choose an alter ego that possesses characteristics you are trying to develop, possibly a different alter ego for your different goals or challenges. Pick a famous or fictional person or invert your cognitive distortions to flesh out a character, and name them appropriately. Find a way to bring that alter ego to life by asking what they would do and taking concrete action accordingly. Alternatively ask for their help or advice, or simply talk about your problem in third person.
- Uncertainty is a part of life, but people vary in their tolerance of it. We can learn to be more tolerant of the unknown outside our comfort zone by acting "as if" we already are. First

identify uncertainty-avoidance behaviors (for example, reassurance seeking), rank them in order of how anxious they make you, then practice each one, tracking your progress.
- When we externalize our anxiety, it has less power over us. Put distance between yourself and your anxious experience so you can see a clearer alternate perspective.
- Narrative therapy can help you externalize. Place the anxiety outside yourself, label it, visualize it, and anchor into your values and goals and see how anxiety jeopardizes them.
- Try to make meaning of your experience, and see if you can create a redeeming narrative according to your own values.

Part Five: Smart Stress Management Tools

Chapter 12: Mind Mapping

As you get better at managing and working with your own anxiety, you will improve your ability to discern between "good stress" and "bad stress." You will be able to identify when your stress is alerting you to a healthy limit or reminding you to take a break or be cautious. You will know when your hesitation has a rational basis and when it is just a bad old habit you learned long ago. Once you have reached this point, it becomes necessary to learn how to manage ordinary, everyday stress. In this chapter, we'll be looking at a few skills and techniques to master as you learn to deal with the stressors of daily life.

You might associate mind maps with studying for exams. But they're also a great way to improve mental health and a tool that can help find clarity and calm. A mind map does exactly what it sounds like it does: helps you **put down in black and white a map of your current mind. It's yet another way to externalize anxiety.**

Imagine you are anxious one day. The feeling comes on slowly and then suddenly. It's hard to say what it is exactly, or where it's coming from. You just know it feels bad. There's a jumble of unpleasant physical sensations, and weird feelings of discomfort seem to blur the lines between physical, mental, and emotional. There are thoughts whizzing around in your head, but they start and don't finish, and they leap from one to the other without any rhyme or reason. In other words, it's a mess.

This is where a mind map comes in—it helps you take a snapshot of that mess so you can untangle it and reflect on what's going on. Any time you find yourself asking,

"Why do I feel this way?"

"What's wrong with me?"

"What's happening to me?"

. . . then it's time to slow down and make a mind map. Here's how.

Step 1: Notice how your body feels

What physical sensations are you experiencing? Slow down and give them a name and locate them in your body. Too many of us have spent a lifetime ignoring what happens from our neck down. We stop registering the information sent to us from our senses, and we become numb to physical signals of stress.

Let's say you get home from work one day and you feel really, really weird. You can't put your finger on it, only you know it feels awful and you want it to stop. You sit down with a piece of A4 paper and write in the middle "How do I feel?" and draw a circle around it. You then draw a branch from there and label it "body." From that branch, you note: *strange nauseous feeling, tight shoulders, pins and needles sensation over the top of skull, dry mouth*, and so on. This is noting, however—not judging, diagnosing, or assuming.

Step 2: Notice areas of tension

If your life itself was a body, where would it be tight right now? Let's say you draw another arm and label this "concerns." What is capturing your attention most at this moment? In the height of panic, it will feel like four thousand things. That's okay—keep drawing another branch and list them all out. Eventually, you will feel like you've put everything down. There's no way to do it wrong, so don't overthink it.

In our example, let's say you note down *discomfort around relationship with sister, worries about drinking too much, overwhelm at work, unsure what to do about event on Saturday, feelings that the world is going to end, irritation with what colleague said*, and so on. For now, just identify broad areas of concern that pop into your mind immediately.

Step 3: Get specific

If you ask the stressed mind what is wrong, it will yell, "Only everything!" But a calmer mind is able to see that only some things are a problem, if they are indeed a problem at all. So look at your mind map as it is and try to whittle down the general areas of concern to more detailed issues. In our example, "feelings that the world is going to end" is actually a definite response you had to watching a doom-and-gloom news report just twenty minutes earlier. It was about how some governments collect recycling but secretly dump it without recycling it. In the moment, you panicked and catastrophized. But when you slow down and take a closer look, there was *one specific thought* that triggered this general feeling. So on your map, you draw a line from that general sensation to something more specific: "feeling alarmed by a news report about recycling."

For the concern "worries about drinking too much," you notice that this was also a specific thought that triggered the general fear that you were drinking too much. You came home, felt tired and overwhelmed, and then thought, *I need a drink.* That was instantly followed by the thought "What if I'm a terrible alcoholic?" Dwelling on this point, you realize that your fear is about how you might seem to others, and you draw another branch: "fear that people will think I'm an alcoholic."

In this way, you move through each area of concern. Some will already be rather specific (such as a comment from a colleague), but some will need some refinement. You may in fact notice that certain areas are strongly connected to one another, or that what you thought was one issue is on second thoughts more like two.

Step 4: Analyze your mind map

You'll eventually reach a point where you can't put much more down without repeating yourself. Then it's time to assess what you've written. First, try to connect the thoughts, feelings, and areas of concern with the physical sensations you experienced. See if you can find patterns. Try to put things in an ordered sequence. Are certain ideas/sensations/thoughts clumped together?

In our example, maybe you notice that there was a definite order of events: first you got home after a stressful day, and then you wanted a drink (and felt guilty about it), and then you turned on the TV to relax but instead saw the distressing news report, and then all at once, the stress of the day seemed to explode into one all-encompassing negative feeling: "The world is going to end." You see how the bodily expression of this feeling is that sense of nausea and neck tension. Gradually, you are drawing a comprehensive map of your experience.

Then what? What do you do after you've mapped your experience this way? The original question in the middle of our mind map was "How do I feel?" After taking a few minutes to create this mind map, it may be clearer to you: You're overwhelmed. This thought "the world is ending" is actually a culmination of many smaller stresses and demands. Slowing down allows you to see that. You can go back in time and piece together exactly where this feeling started, how it built throughout the day, and how it was finally created in the end, like a wave.

Now that you know what you feel, you can do something about it!

If you are overwhelmed, the solution is to reduce stress, stop, and pause and consider only the next step rather than the next twenty steps. Your solution will maybe depend on a little self-care or a well-earned break. What was an undefined brain mess a few moments ago is now clearer and more structured. Ask yourself the following questions to help you further analyze the picture you've created:

- Are there any overlaps with this current experience and experiences you've had before?

- Is there a connecting theme between all your areas of concern?
- Can you see the same cognitive distortion playing out across these areas of concern?
- Is it possible to link up separate sensations and thoughts to show cause and effect?

Now look at the initial question again and see if you can answer it.

Step 5: Make a resolution

Remember the power of action. Your mind map is there to generate insights, but those insights only have power if you can translate them into change in the real world. In our example, you might come to the conclusion that you need to go easier on yourself that evening, and that you need to start making some changes at work to reduce overwhelm. You may decide that you need to have a conversation with your colleague, or that it's time to just let the feud with your sister go. You might implement a new time management system at work or tighten a boundary. Maybe you do something simple like commit to getting eight hours of sleep a night that week or double check that you don't have a vitamin or mineral deficiency.

In the process of determining what actions you can take, try to keep a clear idea of what is actually in your zone of control. Ask yourself: out of these areas of concern, what can I realistically control, and what is outside my control? Then target your efforts to those things you can control, while mustering as much acceptance as possible for those things you can't. You might realize, for example, that you are not singlehandedly responsible for your entire country's recycling policy, but you *are* in control of what you buy and how you throw it away, so you focus on that.

By regularly using mind maps, you can gain a finer, more detailed understanding of what is happening to you. Instead of simply saying "I'm anxious" or "I'm stressed," you can start to say more useful things like "I'm overworked and need a break," "I need a moment to process a feeling of loss," or "I've let my expectations get the better of me."

Most of us, even those who don't suffer anxiety, find the modern world overwhelming. If we don't regularly pause to process, untangle, and work through our emotions, they simply become bigger and more chaotic until they force us to stop. Think of a mind map as a way to do a kind of daily mental spring cleaning and checkup. **You need to give yourself time to reflect, to digest, and to adjust your attitude**, rather than running on some invisible rat wheel, disconnected from how you feel and living reactively.

Daily Anxiety Self-Care

You don't have to wait until you're having a difficult day to draw up a mind map. You might like to do one regularly. This has a few benefits, one of which is that you can see the difference between easier days and more challenging ones and can gain a broader insight into your bigger patterns. For example, you might begin to notice cycles that go over weeks, months, or even years. Maybe you notice that anxiety is worse for you during winter, or especially acute on Fridays. Maybe you notice that when you regularly mind map and "clear your head," you feel a lot calmer and happier the next day.

Mind mapping can also be combined with any of the written techniques we've discussed already. Use your mind map to help you uncover the anxiety cycle as it unfolds for you, or point you in the direction of an unhelpful core belief or cognitive distortion. Use it to give shape to an ABCDE process, where each branch is dedicated to antecedent, behavior, consequence, and so on. Or you could even incorporate elements of externalization and ritual into your mind mapping. For example, you could put your thoughts down on paper and then crumple up or burn it when you're done to symbolize how you have processed those thoughts and are moving on.

Stress is a constant part of life, but it's up to us to regularly keep it at bay, in the same way we clean our homes, shop for groceries, or stay on top of the bills. The trick is that if we address tensions and snags early on when they are still small, we give ourselves the chance to fix them before they turn into enormous, overwhelming crises!

What would you like your daily anxiety self-care to look like?

- Some good heart-pumping exercise and plenty of sweating
- Yoga, stretching, and deep breathing
- A good nutritious meal eaten mindfully
- Some quiet time to reflect, journal, and doodle . . . almost like a "brain dump"
- Reading

- Engaging in a pleasant hobby
- Enjoying a delicious treat
- Listening to music
- Watching a stupid comedy
- Snuggling a pet or loved one
- Having a restorative nap
- Making art
- Going for a gentle walk somewhere beautiful
- Praying or meditating
- Having an indulgent bath and taking your time with grooming

These are all the things we know help us better manage our stress levels, but they work best when they are chosen *strategically* and because we have understood for ourselves why we need them. Too many people have forced themselves to have decadent bubble baths that they hate or pushed ahead with yoga when this actually just bores and annoys them. There is no right or wrong way to relax and release stress, but the best way for you will be something that directly addresses your experience and should never be copied from someone else's lifestyle.

Chapter 13: Better Decision-Making Means Less Anxiety

Too Much Choice

Barry Schwartz is a professor of social theory and social action at Swarthmore College. He also authored the book *The Paradox of Choice: Why More is Less* and is now well-known for his TED Talk on the puzzle of how more choices isn't always better. **Schwartz states that while having a choice is great, having too many options can be overwhelming**. When we are overloaded with choice, the effect is not liberation but a feeling of anxiety, stress, and depression.

The paradox he talks about is how, when we have too many options, we actually tend to act less, make poorer decisions, or become immobilized and demoralized.

Even worse, we blame ourselves for being indecisive or procrastinating, or we are hard on ourselves when our expectations are so distorted that we cannot help being disappointed when we finally do choose something. One phenomenon Schwartz is clear in pointing out is the modern FOMO—or fear of missing out. Even when we do our best to choose wisely, we can never shake the feeling that the other option might have been better, and that we're missing out by not having chosen it.

"Overchoice" was coined by futurist author Alvin Tofler in 1970 in his book *Future Shock*. He explained how people's decision-making processes can be adversely affected by too much choice. It would seem that, as our options grow and expand, so do the possibilities for a potential wrong choice. We may find ourselves paralyzed in our effort to make the very best possible choice—or experience regret.

You'll know that an overabundance of choices is behind your anxiety if:

- You find it difficult to make decisions, and even when you do, you worry about whether you made the right one

- You feel obliged to thoroughly explore all possible options before acting, and can never be spontaneous—and this wastes enormous amounts of your time
- You sometimes feel overwhelmed by the constant need to *optimize*
- You often get so flustered with how much there is on offer that you end up not making a choice at all, or going without something you want or need
- When experiencing something new, you tend to find it overwhelming, confusing, or stressful, rather than exciting or pleasant
- You sometimes miss out on opportunities because you're afraid of taking a leap of faith and acting without perfect knowledge of how it will turn out

How to Use "Fear-Setting"

Author, speaker, and productivity guru Tim Ferris has written at length about the technique he calls fear-setting. **This is a method of making life decisions based on your fears rather than your goals**. It might sound counterintuitive, but the power of this approach is that it gives you a broader perspective (is what you're afraid of really such a big deal?) and helps you identify risk-mitigation strategies that actually do something about it.

By implementing fear-setting, you can save energy you would have used worrying about insignificant decisions and funnel it into those big-deal decisions that really do matter. Ferris loves the quote from Seneca the Younger: "We suffer more in imagination than in reality." With fear-setting, you commit to suffering no more than you should, so you can get back to the real work of managing reality.

Set aside thirty minutes to one hour and get three pages of A4 paper ready. On the first page, you are taking a magnifying glass to your fears and looking at them closely, rather than shying away from them. On the first page, draw out three columns with the following headings:

Define
Prevent
Repair

In the first column (define), describe in clear terms whatever it is you fear about taking a certain action. This is the place for your catastrophic visions of failures, doubts, or terrifying "what if" outcomes. You're fully exploring the worst-case scenario. For example, if you're afraid of launching your own business, you might note every fear you have that's holding you back, from bankruptcy to judgment from family to never getting a weekend off again.

In the second column (prevent), write down ways that you could lower the chances of each of those things happening. Big or small, note these actions down. For example, you could take a business management class, launch your new venture slowly rather than all at once, seek a mentor, make some time-management goals, etc.

In the third column (repair), list out all the things you could do if the worst came to pass anyway. What damage control could you do? For example, even if you did completely bomb financially, what could you do to get back on track? Even if your family wasn't supportive, where else could you find support?

To finish this first part of the exercise, look again at all these worst-case scenarios and assess their impact on your life. How much of a setback would it realistically be? You could say a score of one was a minor impact, whereas ten was life-altering and significant. In our example, a lack of support from others is bad but not the end of the world, and you might rate it five out of ten. Bankruptcy is a lot worse, and you might say it's around nine out of ten.

Okay, great, but you're not done yet! Take out the second page. Page one was about looking at the costs of taking action. Page two is going to be about measuring the *benefits* of that same action. This alone is quite the perspective shift—how often do you ruminate over all the things that could go right with a new course of action?

Make a list of all possible benefits—and not just if the outcome is a major success, either. List out benefits of simply having tried, or a partial success. For instance, even if you launch a new business and it fails completely, you have gained valuable information by trying it out and seeing that it didn't work. If you imagine that you're a scientist, *any* outcome is valuable because it reveals information that you cannot access in any other way.

Other benefits could include a boost in confidence (You did it! You felt the fear and did it anyway!) and also the realization that what you feared was not really that scary after all. Anxiety can paralyze you, but if you take action in the right direction, even a small step can break you out of that rut and get you thinking of new solutions and new alternatives. That momentum can be valuable, even if the single step itself did not go as planned.

Finally, you might meet new people, learn a new skill, or uncover a very serious limitation you weren't aware of before (an often unappreciated gift of failing early!). When you try, you immediately avoid that sinking feeling of always wondering what would have happened if you had just ignored your fear and done it. When you're anxious, you seldom think about it, but avoiding regret has a lot of value in the long run.

Finally, as you did on page one, rate the potential benefits of these successes on a ten-point scale. A little boost to the confidence might be rated four out of ten, while actually achieving one of your major life goals would max out the scale at ten out of ten.

You can probably guess what page three is going to be about! Here, you are considering the *cost of not acting*. Because yes, there is one! Your fear is an evolutionary response designed to keep you safe. But it also frequently errs on the side of caution. It may be giving you a "false positive," which means it is telling you that something is risky and dangerous when it isn't. When you are anxious, all you can focus on is what you are avoiding in that moment. The temporary pain or embarrassment. The awkwardness of being a beginner or having to find your feet. If you act to avoid those feelings, it can seem in the moment like you've gained something . . . but what have you lost?

On page three, again draw three columns, labeled six months, one year, and three years. This is because the biggest costs for inaction are usually longer term (while our fear is limited to the present). Now, fill out each column with an anticipated cost of not acting, as it may play out over three years. In other words, what happens to you if you do nothing and just maintain the status quo?

List out emotional, financial, physical, and even spiritual or social impacts.

In our example, not starting your own business when you've dreamed of it your whole life may have profound consequences—most of them only revealed in the long term. You may feel safe in the short term, but as the months and years roll by, you may get bored and uninspired with your current job. It may feel safe and predictable but constricting.

You may start to gradually lose a little faith in yourself. After all, if even *you* don't believe in your vision, it's as though you lower your reputation with yourself. You come to expect less of yourself and take fewer risks, doing less and less to challenge yourself. Consequently you may feel a little regretful or have dampened self-esteem. When you see others achieving what you wanted to, you might feel envious or bitter. If you had succeeded in the business, you may have made far more money than you do now . . . and over time, that money would grow, leaving you at a very different place three years on. Staying in the same job, however, may instead mean an income that doesn't grow all that much over time.

For many people, the work done on this page amounts to: "If I do nothing, my life stays the same—or it gradually gets worse."

Now, if you are perfectly happy with where you are, then this shouldn't matter. But if you have ambitions for yourself, unfulfilled potential, curiosity, a hunger to learn, or a desire to improve yourself, then this should give you a fresh perspective. Not acting seems like "doing nothing." But it's not—it's a choice. Ask yourself at the end of page three if the status quo is something you are *actively* choosing.

Once you have completed all three pages, take a look again at what you are afraid of. You should now have a lot more clarity and understanding about how this fear fits into your life—what it is protecting you from, but also what it is costing you. As we've said, not all fear is irrational. This exercise will drive home clearly for you which fears are genuinely serving you and which are only holding you back.

Done often enough, such a mindset shift may slowly convince you that trying to avoid the things you are most afraid of can cause a lot of damage, whereas facing them head on is usually not as bad as you predicted. Anxiety and fear keep you in the status quo. Avoidance behaviors feel safe and comfy for a time, but they very seldom create positive change in anyone's life.

Maybe you have a concern that is actually realistic and healthy. In our example, let's say your business idea is to start an online psychotherapy platform for pet hamsters, and you plan to quit your current job immediately to pursue it, despite knowing nothing about psychology, online businesses, or hamsters. Wouldn't it be appropriate in that case to have a little self-doubt and fear?

Actually, no. Rumination, worry, and anxiety are never really useful. Overvaulting confidence and recklessness isn't useful, either. What this exercise does is ask you to take emotion out of it entirely and **base your actions on conscious, informed choice.** If you consider the situation carefully and decide that the status quo is the best option after all, do so not because you are afraid of acting, but because you are consciously choosing not to. In other words, try to abandon the idea that anxiety equals carefulness. You can be cautious, shrewd, and well-informed without needing an ounce of anxiety.

The Value-Based Strategy

Any time you put conscious, informed action in place of driving your life rather than fear, you empower yourself. The same can be said for making decisions based on what you value, rather than what you're afraid of.

Using a value-based decision-making process means you "live and breathe" what you care about and infuse everything you do with a chosen end point in mind. Too often, anxiety erodes our sense of dignity and purpose because it forces us to focus on the negative and everything we don't want, don't like, or are afraid of. But when we ask the question "What do I really want?" we flip this on its head.

When you do so, a lot of extraneous information falls away because it's simply not relevant to you. For example, imagine your values are all about personal fulfilment and integrity. You feel good when you live up to your own standards. If you then have the anxious thought *What will everyone think of me? What if they judge me?* you can immediately run it through the filter of your values and see that it is largely irrelevant—it doesn't matter what other people think because that's not what you're about or the main motivator for your behavior. So, **it's easier to shrug off these doubts and fears and re-focus on your own personal fulfilment and integrity**.

So what do you value? It may be:

Excellence
Learning and knowledge
Family life
Spiritual pursuits
Kindness and harmony
Art and creativity
Hard work
Financial security
Independence
Novelty and exploration
Peace and tranquility
Fame and influence
Romance
Good health and fitness
Mastery in a skill

Wouldn't you like these things to be in the driver's seat of your life?

The next time you find yourself feeling fearful, full of self-doubt, or even just lazy, ask whether your actions and attitude align with your highest values. Does the company you want to work at align with those values? Do the friends and relationships you have make it easier for you to live those values? Does your speech, attitude, and behavior flow from these values? Ask these questions and you are allowing yourself to be guided toward something good rather than merely escaping something bad. It's aspirational, not evasive.

Good questions to ask yourself:

What can I learn from this choice?
What information don't I have and how could I go about getting it?
How can I actively test my assumptions?
What would a person with my values choose to do?
Which options can I dismiss as irrelevant?
What is the smallest risk-free action I can take to get moving again?

Chapter 14: Turning Your Anxiety into a Superpower

Wendy Suzuki is a neuroscientist and the author of *Good Anxiety: Harnessing the Power of the Most Misunderstood Emotion*. She believes that **one of the best things you can do is to stop thinking of your anxiety as some debilitating disability and start appreciating its potential as a positive motivating force in your life**. With a little patience, acceptance, and conscious awareness, she believes anyone can take their anxious tendencies and turn them to their advantage.

We'll repeat here, however, that this in no way undermines the value of properly treating and even medicating anxiety if it has become sever enough in your life to warrant it. Nevertheless, all of us possess some ability to take charge of our anxiety, manage it, mitigate it, and, in some circumstances, use it to help us achieve the things we actually want.

Think about what anxiety is without any value judgment: It's energy.

When you are nervous, fidgety, alert, hyperfocused, and burning with the desire to DO SOMETHING, it doesn't take much to see how such a state of mind can be valuable. Suzuki calls anxiety "the superpower of productivity," provided you can harness it. You want to keep the energy and drive of anxiety while paying close attention to the *content* of your worries. Think of your anxiety as a wild horse. With a little training and steering, you can make it go in the direction you choose.

Suzuki wants to remind us what our anxiety was originally *for*—what its evolutionary purpose is. It's simple: **Anxiety is meant to keep you alert to real threats in the environment and make sure that you have enough energy and focus to make a plan to keep yourself safe from that threat**. That's a wonderful adaptation! So, let's not be in too much of a hurry to get rid of our anxiety forever, lest we also forego the power to focus, to be energized and motivated, and to think on our feet to make smart, proactive plans to move forward.

Instead of trying to "treat" anxiety or get rid of it, Suzuki thinks we should respect and appreciate it and learn to work with it as much as we can. "Like a sailboat needs wind in order to move, the brain-body needs an outside force to urge it to grow, adapt, and not die," she says in her book. She claims there are in fact six superpowers we get if we can learn to reclaim anxiety rather than constantly try to push it away. These include the ability to:

- Strengthen your overall physical and emotional resilience
- Perform tasks and activities at a higher level
- Optimize and fine tune your mindset
- Increase your focus and productivity
- Enhance your social intelligence
- Improve your creative skills

Instead of "Resilience," Adopt the "Activist Mindset"

Let's start with the past. If you are currently struggling with issues and worries, try to **think back to similar emotional trials and tribulations that you have already come through**. What insights can you glean? Can you turn the fact of that past adversity into a reason to feel more confident in your abilities today? Can you see how a little of the same creativity and open-mindedness might help you overcome whatever hurdle you're facing right now?

If you can learn to adopt what Suzuki calls an active mindset, "you become able to assert more top-down control of your attitude and orientation toward the bad, uncomfortable feelings associated with anxiety, shifting both your experience of the bad feelings and your belief that you can channel them in positive ways."

For example, if you are in the middle of an anxious moment, you might be thinking, *I don't know how I'm going to do this. I'm scared. I don't know what I'm doing. What if this, what if that . . .*

But if you are in an activist mindset, you can look back and say, "I have already felt this way before. I managed and survived. In fact, I did a pretty good job then, even though I was scared." It's about reframing.

Negative Feelings Are Not a Problem

You don't have to keep reframing everything until it looks good—that would be unrealistic! You are never required to mask your true feelings or pretend that everything's just peachy. In fact, Suzuki thinks that the negativity is part of what gives anxiety its value, so don't be in too much of a hurry to slap on a smile and hide your fear. "**The negative aspect is what's protective—it's critical**. Those feelings are there to help direct us to what we value. We want to feel them and learn from them, rather than being beaten down by them," she says.

Again, it's a mindset shift from "this anxiety is a problem, so I have to solve it immediately" to "well, why is this anxiety here? What function is it serving? What is it trying to tell me?" One is a passive, defensive approach, whereas the other is the "activist" one that puts you back in charge. Imagine someone is experiencing anxiety around their job and work life. They constantly have indigestion and poor sleep, racing thoughts, tight muscles, and fears and self-doubts that border on catastrophic. But if that person rushes in to medicate those feelings, cover them up with "mindfulness exercises," or positive thinking, then they may have lost a precious opportunity for insight: that they are overdue some big changes in their work!

Suzuki writes about her own life and learning to see where anxiety was acting as a flashing warning light. When she ignored this warning and pressed on, trying to appear happy and energetic, she actually ended up feeling lonely, disconnected from her purpose, and even more anxious. The warning bell kept sounding louder and louder. Instead, she found relief when she asked her anxiety, "What are you showing me?" and discovered that it had some valuable lessons to teach her about what was missing from her life.

So, don't be afraid of negative emotions or anxiety. Of course, you shouldn't *dwell* on them, either. But put them to good use by asking the purpose they serve and then making a plan to address what they are trying to show you.

Do you need more rest, self-care, and downtime?
Are people violating your boundaries . . . or are *you* doing so?
Are you actually trying to live up to someone else's standards and ideas, rather than your own?
Have you lost authenticity and a connection to your own values and purpose?
Are you doing something you know is wrong?
Are you behaving in a way that is hurting or undermining you?

In our example, anxiety is telling the person that they need to change the way they work or take a real break. Something isn't adding up. Something needs to change. So, before you assume that your anxiety is just some silly thing to discount and ignore, listen to what it says first. It may be silly, but it may also have valuable information for you, if you'd only listen.

Convert Worry to Action

We return to the idea again and again in this book: A worry that is converted into action stops being a worry. **One way to harness the energetic power of your anxiety is to actually give it some work to do.** A wild horse kept pent up in a stable will only get agitated and pace around and around, or perhaps even kick up a fuss and cause damage to itself and to others. But a horse that is saddled and made to work will find a channel for that energy. It can pull a cart or carry someone long distances.

Suzuki recommends taking all your "what if" lists and converting them to "to-do" lists. Make your anxiety earn its keep! You may be sitting late at night with your thoughts going round and round, catastrophizing, thinking of endless doom-and-gloom possibilities. Instead, get specific, get practical, and get active.

Let's say you're worried that the tax return you've just submitted is actually riddled with mistakes. That night, you're unable to sleep as your head fills up with scary what-if scenarios. What if you've completely messed up and you owe way more than you thought you did? What if you've missed something big and it comes back to bite you? What if the mistake is so big that it's actually illegal, and suited men come in the middle of the night to arrest you for tax evasion?

Okay, so pause. Take a deep breath. Yes, even this flurry of anxiety has a purpose and can be put to good use. Instead of trying to meditate yourself to sleep and ignore your fears, face them head on. This anxiety may be trying to help ensure you don't make a costly error. That can be useful. Turn the what if into a list of to-do items. What if you made a mistake? Well, did you? Make a list of actions you can take to literally check, instead of just thinking about it. Be specific: What are you worried you have forgotten about? Drill down until you find the precise thing you're stressing over.

You soon realize there was one question in particular you weren't sure about, and just guessed your response. Okay, fine. Make a to-do list—first thing in the morning, do some online Googling so you fully understand the question and how you are meant to answer it. Then, check that off the list. You don't need to worry about it anymore. You may find that it's actually much, much easier to let go of a worry if you know you have logically taken all the action you can. You're like a wild horse that is tired from work and can finally relax.

Of course, if you look at your what-ifs and can't convert them into action, then you have a host of other skills to allow you to accept them, reframe them, or at the very least distract yourself. Remember the serenity prayer: Grant me the serenity to accept the things I cannot change, the courage to change the things I can, and the wisdom to know the difference. Notice the key that allows you to differentiate? It's **action**—if you can act, act. If you can't, let it go. That wisdom will turn your natural anxiety into a superpower.

Be Ultra-Careful with Your Screen Time

Start to look at your smartphone (or laptop or tablet) as a potential anxiety over-stimulator. You don't need to be gorging on doom-and-gloom news stories for your phone to make you anxious (although it goes without saying that doing so definitely doesn't help!). Remember that your anxiety is a survival adaptation. Your alertness evolved as a way to scan the environment for potential threats. Once your brain is convinced you've done that, you can relax. Accept devices and internet in general short circuit this ability because they create an artificial environment that is constantly updating. Therefore, it needs to be constantly scanned for threats. It's a recipe for useless, non-directed anxiety.

Scrolling mindlessly online creates a sense of urgency and anxiety, with no avenue to discharge that energy. There's nothing to *do* about most of what you encounter online. It creates not only anxiety but a feeling of passivity and distraction. An ongoing onslaught of notifications forces you to multitask, and taxes your executive functioning. The stream of data is infinite— but your cognitive powers are not.

Protect your ability to think deeply, to concentrate with unbroken attention, to brainstorm your own creative ideas and original responses to things, to process, to pause, and to remember. Set hard limits for screen time. The content doesn't matter! "There are a bunch of smart people preying on us by analyzing what we click on and what will make us keep clicking, whether that's Instagram clothes or Instagram bodies or Instagram items that you don't have but want to have," says Suzuki, who recommends that you watch yourself like a hawk—how does screen time actually seep you're your life? Wouldn't you like to put your time, attention, and energy toward something that better fits your goals and values? It's about taking back that control.

Let Go of Your Own Problems and Find Compassion for Other People's

Anxiety has another unexpected gift: the invitation to become a more empathetic, compassionate person:

> "Pay attention to where your anxiety is drawing your attention. Use those moments in your life as a starting point for reaching out to others. If you have anxiety as the new person at work, take the time to talk to the other new hires to make them feel at ease. If you struggle with balancing kids and work, take the time to give a word of encouragement to the other

> new mothers and fathers in your circle."

Here, anxiety can give you insight into other people's experiences—and make you a lot kinder as a result. As an anxious person, you may gain a deeper understanding into the way other people may be struggling. Suzuki gives the example of the nervousness students may feel in lectures when asking a question. But she was able to remember her own experience of being too scared to ask a question in a lecture when she was a student. The anxiety she felt then became a way for her to peak into the minds of her students now, where she was in the role of a lecturer. Her understanding allows her to take useful concrete steps—for example, by letting students know they can come to her privately after lectures to ask questions. Her ability to make this adaptation came directly from her experience of anxiety.

Ask yourself what kind of gestures have made your anxiety better in the past? Then, commit to offering that to other people. It's difficult to overstate how emotionally satisfying this can be. It's a way to process anxiety and make something good of it. Getting into the heads of other people this way can make you instantly more approachable, empathetic, and socially intelligent.

If your anxiety is triggered by a bad memory, counter it by reminding yourself of someone you feel grateful for. Reach out and tell them you're grateful! If you're struggling with something, ask how you can volunteer or donate to a good cause connected to that struggle, and in the process, you empower yourself and others to overcome it. If you are unsure about something, reach out to someone and ask their advice, or ask them to teach you something. You strengthen your relationships while letting them know how much you value their opinion.

Summary:

- Learn to distinguish between good and bad stress. Mind maps are a snapshot of your current mind and can help you externalize anxiety and find clarity. Run a body scan and notice areas of tension, then ask a question and explore different branches on your mind map. Whittle general areas of concern to specific

issues, then analyze and reflect so you can take informed action. Do this as part of your regular self-care routine, not just in crisis.
- If decision-making is causing anxiety, consider if you have too many options. When we have too many options, we actually tend to act less, make poorer decisions, or become immobilized and demoralized, or else suffer from FOMO and blame ourselves for indecision.
- Tim Ferris's fear-setting method is a way to counter overchoice and make life decisions based on your fears rather than your goals. Use three pieces of paper to identify the costs of acting, the benefits of acting, and finally the costs of *not* acting. By ranking and rating these clearly and rationally, you allow yourself to make empowered choices and not be pushed around by fear. Remember that doing nothing is a choice, and that taking a chance is often less scary than we predict it will be.

- Try to keep your values in mind to cut down on extraneous information and push past fear.
- Stop thinking of your anxiety as a debilitating disability, and start appreciating its potential as a positive motivating force in your life. Adopt an activist mindset, think of what you've already achieved, ask what your fear is teaching you, convert worries to actions by making a to-do list, limit screen time, and ask how your own fears can help you become more empathetic toward other people's fears.

Summary Guide

PART ONE: UNDERSTANDING HOW ANXIETY WORKS

- The more anxious you feel, the more afraid you are of that experience, and the more you try to avoid it—but this prevents you from learning about how anxiety operates, and therefore gaining power over it.
- Anxiety follows a familiar path: 1. Something internal or external triggers a fight-or-flight response, 2. Your brain adapts by finding ways to avoid that stimulus (rightly or wrongly), 3. The reward of temporary relief that reinforces the avoidance mechanism, 4. The inevitable return of heightened anxiety. Familiarity with this cycle allow you to check your response and intervene. Try a body scan and reflect on your process.
- Typically, we respond to our *thoughts about a trigger* and not strictly the trigger itself. Reverse the cycle by confronting feared situations without the help of unhealthy coping

mechanisms, then trying healthier alternatives.
- Anxiety is a learned behavior entrenched in habit. Our habit cycles are made of a triggering cue, the behavior itself, and a reward that reinforces it. Slow down and note what your cues and rewards are.
- Understand your anxiety habits and work with your brain rather than against it, replacing bad habits with better ones. Maintain an attitude of curiosity and compassion, and try to replace negative "soundtracks" with more positive or neutral ones.
- Ask if your soundtracks are kind, true, or helpful, and if not, invert them, or take inspiration from the soundtracks of people you admire. Tell yourself: *I have the permission and the ability to choose what I think during the day and to choose the actions I will take.*

PART TWO: UNRAVELING THE ANXIETY RESPONSE

- The fight-or-flight response is one that *narrows perception*, but a timeline exercise can reacquaint you with the bigger picture. Look from the outside to see events with neutral eyes, and move through memories by pausing, rewinding, and fast forwarding to understand how it all comes together.
- Figure out how you have interpreted an event and the meanings you have ascribed to them, then become curious about healthier alternatives. This can also be done to identify long-term anxiety patterns across your whole life.
- "You are disturbed not by things, but the views which you take of them." The ABCDE model helps you identify the activating event, the belief, and the consequences of the belief, as well as identify the possibility of disputing the belief and observing the resulting effect. The method helps us identify our particular interpretations of neutral events and challenge our resulting beliefs about them. We cement new beliefs by applying them

and taking action—so *don't* fake it till you make it.
- The distance between reality and our unrealistic expectations can be a source of anxiety. Consider if your expectations are fair, rational, kind, and useful, and be aware of your idea of reality versus reality.
- Drop the word "should," stop comparing yourself to others, have compassion for yourself, ask for help, and reconnect to your values and principles rather than arbitrary and irrational expectations or standards. Be curious how your core beliefs are informing your expectations of how things should play out.
- Gratitude and emotional acceptance can help you embrace what is and encourage a healthier relationship to reality.

PART THREE: YOUR BRAIN—FRIEND OR FOE?

- Your brain can work against you if it runs on cognitive distortions, which are simply inaccurate pictures of

reality. These can include overgeneralization, black-and-white thinking, emotional reasoning, discounting the positive, catastrophizing, or mind reading. Whatever they are or how they work, distortions are a deliberate misinterpretation of stimuli to serve a conclusion that is negative or threatening. This leads to anxiety.
- The triple column exercise can help you identify and rewrite cognitive distortions, or replace them with something more rational. Note down the 1. Automatic thought, 2. The distortion, and 3. A rational alternative. Walk yourself through each assumption and interpretation and ask for evidence, looking to see if there is another way to frame events.
- Reality testing means making a clear distinction between your own thoughts, hopes, wishes, fears, and ideas about an event and reality itself. Actively look for alternative explanations, dial down assumptions, and look for evidence that counters a

negative automatic reaction to stimuli.
- Look for a neutral, objective perspective; remember that there is a space between a stimulus and your response to it, and that you never *have to* react, so take your time to process; and finally, anchor yourself in alternative and external points of view rather than assuming yours is gospel.
- Being non-anxious is not about living a life free of difficulty. It's a relationship to reality that is clear-sighted, accepting, and realistic.
- Lastly, recognize what anxiety is yours and what belongs to other people. Never substitute someone else's perspective as your own or take responsibility for their emotions or actions.

PART FOUR: TAKING A STEP BACK

- The Batman effect helps us get "psychological distance" from our own limited ideas of who we are and what we are capable of. Working with an alter ego can help us push back against ingrained negative biases we have toward ourselves.
- Choose an alter ego that possesses characteristics you are trying to develop, possibly a different alter ego for your different goals or challenges. Pick a famous or fictional person or invert your cognitive distortions to flesh out a character, and name them appropriately. Find a way to bring that alter ego to life by asking what they would do and taking concrete action accordingly. Alternatively ask for their help or advice, or simply talk about your problem in third person.
- Uncertainty is a part of life, but people vary in their tolerance of it. We can learn to be more tolerant of the unknown outside our comfort zone by acting "as if" we already are. First identify uncertainty-avoidance behaviors (for example, reassurance seeking), rank them in order of how anxious they make you, then practice each one, tracking your progress.

- When we externalize our anxiety, it has less power over us. Put distance between yourself and your anxious experience so you can see a clearer alternate perspective.
- Narrative therapy can help you externalize. Place the anxiety outside yourself, label it, visualize it, and anchor into your values and goals and see how anxiety jeopardizes them.
- Try to make meaning of your experience, and see if you can create a redeeming narrative according to your own values.

PART FIVE: SMART STRESS MANAGEMENT TOOLS

- Learn to distinguish between good and bad stress. Mind maps are a snapshot of your current mind and can help you externalize anxiety and find clarity. Run a body scan and notice areas of tension, then ask a question and explore different branches on your mind map. Whittle

general areas of concern to specific issues, then analyze and reflect so you can take informed action. Do this as part of your regular self-care routine, not just in crisis.
- If decision-making is causing anxiety, consider if you have too many options. When we have too many options, we actually tend to act less, make poorer decisions, or become immobilized and demoralized, or else suffer from FOMO and blame ourselves for indecision.
- Tim Ferris's fear-setting method is a way to counter overchoice and make life decisions based on your fears rather than your goals. Use three pieces of paper to identify the costs of acting, the benefits of acting, and finally the costs of *not* acting. By ranking and rating these clearly and rationally, you allow yourself to make empowered choices and not be pushed around by fear. Remember that doing nothing is a choice, and that taking a chance is often less scary than we predict it will be.

- Try to keep your values in mind to cut down on extraneous information and push past fear.
- Stop thinking of your anxiety as a debilitating disability, and start appreciating its potential as a positive motivating force in your life. Adopt an activist mindset, think of what you've already achieved, ask what your fear is teaching you, convert worries to actions by making a to-do list, limit screen time, and ask how your own fears can help you become more empathetic toward other people's fears.

www.ingramcontent.com/pod-product-compliance
Lightning Source LLC
Chambersburg PA
CBHW020527080526
44583CB00013B/762